You Can't See Me, But I'm Here

A haunting in Centrahoma

A TRUE AND PERSONAL ACCOUNT OF
PARANORMAL ACTIVITY IN SOUTHERN
OKLAHOMA, DURING THE YEARS 1997
THROUGH 2003 AS WITNESSED BY;

JASON R. TAYLOR

authorHOUSE™

1663 LIBERTY DRIVE, SUITE 200
BLOOMINGTON, INDIANA 47403
(800) 839-8640
WWW.AUTHORHOUSE.COM

First published by AuthorHouse 05/12/05

ISBN: 1-4208-5159-4 (sc)

Printed in the United States of America
Bloomington, Indiana

This book is printed on acid-free paper.

PROLOGUE,

OVER THE YEARS MANY SCIENTISTS BELIEVED, IF YOU COULDN'T SEE IT OR FEEL IT, THEN IT MUST NOT BE REAL.

I BEG TO DIFFER,

JASON R. TAYLOR

PREFACE

You Can't See Me, But I'm Here is an account of my personal experiences in an old house in southeastern Oklahoma. The house is known locally, because of the bizarre events which take place there. The house is the Mcwethy family home.

The Mcwethy's lived in the house since 1983, without incident until one hot summer evening in June of 1990, when life in the house took a dramatic turn. Someone or something, unseen by the occupants began to harass and torment the family, and those who visit the house.

This book is about the events I personally witnessed at the house, the reactions of those who were present, and the lasting affects that these experiences have had on my life.

For years after my first encounter with the house, I could not stop thinking about what I had witnessed there, and for that reason this book was born. I wrote this book because I felt compelled to write it, out of shear curiosity, and a persistent desire to solve the mystery of the house, and thereby to finally find peace in my own life.

In loving memory of my father,
Clarence Emory "Hank" Taylor
January 7, 1938 – March 25th 2004.
Now with God, and never will be forgotten.

A SPECIAL THANKS TO ROBERT FISCHER, FOR WITHOUT HIS TIRELESS HELP AND COMMITMENT TO THIS PROJECT, THIS BOOK WOULD NOT HAVE BEEN POSSIBLE.

ONE

It was mid November 1996, while working the late shift at a local grocery store, that I finally decided it was time to move on. The store I was employed with was part of a large grocery chain on the Oregon coast. I had worked at my present job as a grocery clerk for a little over a year. The job that I had held was fast becoming stressful because of the late hours, and a sleep pattern that would not satisfy a cat. Before this job, I had worked as a waiter at my parent's café and as a desk clerk at a local Motel, where I sold rooms. At that time in my life, I lived in a small coastal village along the Oregon coast.

For some reason I could not stick with a job for more than a year however, I think that reason was because I would get bored with any type of repetition. My good friend Wayne once told me, I needed to settle down and stay with something whether I liked it or not.

While I was working that night, I began to reflect on my childhood.

I grew up in a large family setting in the sixties and seventies living a modest lifestyle. We resided north of Reno, Nevada in a newly built tract of homes, at the base of the mountains. I lived with my Stepfather George, Mother Gwen, Sister Kelly, and three brothers, Guy, Jeff, and Tracy. George my Stepfather was the disciplinarian in the home; George was a military man and wanted everything neat and tidy, while My Mother kept the family together. Mom on the other hand, was easy going and did not sweat the small stuff.

While in my early teens, I ran away from home a few times, not because I was unhappy living at home, but because I wanted to travel and see the world. My parents did not realize it at the time, but they were raising a vagabond.

Mom and Dad used to take us to Mexico for vacations in the summer, after school let out. We drove in an old station wagon on vacation, which allowed me plenty of time for looking out the windows as every town we passed, made me want to travel more.

I moved to Oregon in May of 1990, shortly after my wife Jeannie and I divorced. Jeannie and I fell in love as high school sweethearts and worked at the same retail store. After our divorce, I decided I wanted to live in Oregon so I could be closer to my Dad Hank, Stepmother Patricia, and three stepsisters, Edith, Pauline, and Sherry.

So there I was in the store late at night, busting my ass for a meager living, when I realized it was time for a change. And why not? I was single, and had no responsibilities and no children to raise. A change of scenery sounded good. Suddenly, I felt flush and nervous, all at the same time. Telling the store manager Rick of my plans would not be easy, as he was a good friend of mine, and my boss. Rick would not understand my reasons for leaving, mainly because he believed that if you had a job, any job, you should stick with it no matter what the circumstances. The only job Rick ever had was the Grocery store.

Rick, the store manager, was a short husky fellow with red hair, a good sense of humor, and a strong work ethic.

I started to get nervous about six that morning, knowing Rick would be in soon. I did a good job for Rick and I knew he would not want to lose me.

My Dad and Stepmother owned a small, but successful restaurant down in the old part of town. The restaurant was small and cozy, and a favorite of the locals. I had worked at the restaurant as a waiter, before going to work at the grocery store.

Rick came in the store shortly after six a.m. in a good mood. He approached me after he walked around the store, and thanked me for the way the store looked. It was my job to make sure the shelves were faced, the floors were clean and the front end ready for the new day. "No problem" I said, "by the way, could I speak with you for a moment?" By the look on his face, I could tell he knew what was coming, well, he was right.

I explained to Rick that it was time for me to move on to other things. At that moment, his face turned red and he gave me a look I had not seen in a long time. Rick said with an angry smirk on his face, "I need you"; I don't understand why you want to leave". I told Rick I was sorry he was upset, but I was leaving and that was all that needed to be said.

During the time Rick and I spoke that morning; I also mentioned that Tracy, my brother lived in Oklahoma, and he wanted me to move there.

I left my job at the store on November 30, 1996 moreover, planned to move to Oklahoma, on the fourth, of December.

The night I was to leave for Oklahoma my family threw me a going away party; I think they were just trying to get rid of me in a nice way, Just kidding, I knew they would miss me.

At about eight o'clock that evening, after the party, I left for Oklahoma. As I left the Southern Oregon Coast and headed inland to interstate 5, I felt empty inside, as though I had lost a certain direction in my life. As I drove, loneliness began to set in, knowing that I would not see my brother Tracy, or his family, for at least two days.

Once in the state of California, the rain began to fall. All I could think about was getting to Oklahoma, almost as though someone or something was pushing me like the wind pushes leaves from a tree after they have fallen. As darkness began to fade and my eyes became heavy, I soon realized that nine straight hours of driving were beginning to take a toll on my mind and body.

The weather began to cool rapidly as I crossed into Arizona. As I traveled through the desert of Arizona, coming down from the mountains, I noticed small buildings that were Native American shops. I stopped to look at some arts and crafts and found they were way out of my price range; however, they had some nice Indian crafts I would have liked to have.

By the time I reached the New Mexico border at about two in the morning, I was exhausted. The sky was clear but it was cold outside, and I needed to stop and get some sleep.

It was about eight o'clock the next morning as I drove through the Oklahoma State line knowing the trip was just about over. I pulled to the side of the road to see if I could map out a short route to the small town of Fletcher.

Deciding to get out and stretch my legs, my body was overcome by the bitter cold of the Midwest. This was going to take some getting used to as Oregon offered a much milder climate, not withstanding the ninety-mile an hour wind and rainstorms. I also had to contend with the fact that I was in Tornado country where at any given time, a community could be ripped in half. Tornados are Mother Nature's way of saying I am not prejudice, I will wreak havoc on any one, place, or thing, but as I would later discover, having something thrown at you from out of nowhere, would prove to be far worse. If you see something coming, you can react to the threat, but to have several different items thrown at you from something you cannot see, you are in serious trouble.

The sun had been up for about six hours as I pulled into the small rural community of Fletcher, but it was still cold outside. I had already gotten directions to Tracy's house while still in Oregon. As I pulled into the driveway, I noticed the front door to the house wide open, and as I got out of the car, I could hear the sound of children screaming. I thought to myself, Yep, this is the right house.

At the time, Tracy and his wife Tammy, had seven children, Justin, Chris, Corey, Jennifer, Caitlin, Jason, and Jessica.

As I walked to the front door, I was met by Tammy, Tracy's wife, who did not look a day older since I had last seen her. Tammy was a petite woman with shoulder length brown hair and nice disposition.

Tracy and Tammy had been married for about thirteen years and seemed to get along well. We hugged and said our hello's and went in the house. I could not see Tracy, as Tammy then told me he was at work. She explained that he would be home later. The children were all home and I was introduced to them one by one, I had only met two of their children several years back.

Tracy arrived home about an hour after I had gotten to the house. As he walked into the living room where Tammy and I had been talking, I got up and gave him a hug. I could not believe how well built he was; I remembered he was always exercising when we were younger.

Tracy and I looked a lot alike moreover, our voices sounded eerily similar. When we were kid's we did everything together, including getting into trouble, which we were good at doing. We fought often as young children mainly, because we shared a room together. I would keep my side of the room clean, and he would deliberately mess his side up, just to cause trouble However, we were still good friends as well as siblings.

We spoke for about an hour before I decided to get some much-needed sleep, we would continue our catching up the next day.

That next morning Tammy asked me when I was going to look for employment, Tracy intervened and said, "He just got here, let him relax". We were all excited that the holidays were coming, and could spend them together.

Two weeks had gone by before I started looking for work; money was tight as I tried to find out if I could get Unemployment benefits. I checked and found out I could get a good amount weekly, However that would not last long. Right away, I was receiving Unemployment benefits and stopped looking for employment. Tracy wanted me to help with the two youngest children until I found work. Tammy was going to college full time at the University of Oklahoma, and Tracy was serving in the Army at Fort Sill, Oklahoma. I had no problem helping watch the kids because I was not yet working.

Christmas morning dawned and as expected, the kids were up early, with smiles on their faces as they opened all those gifts. The living room floor was littered with torn paper and partially opened presents. They got some cool toys, which I enjoyed playing with.

Tammy cooked breakfast and then a large dinner that night, which for me, was the first Christmas dinner with close family in years.

During the next few weeks, I was watching the children often as Tammy was in school and Tracy at work. Stressed and annoyed with my situation at the house, I knew I had to get a job. I was resigned to the fact that stress, in any form, was unhealthy for me.

The next day I went into Lawton, which at the time, was the third largest city in Oklahoma, and began looking for work. Every place I checked met with the same answer, to slow or wrong time of year, still I was determined to persevere.

Two days later, I was able to go back to Lawton and continue looking for a job, with God hopefully on my side I would find employment. I was not a religious person by any stretch; my theory was simply, if I were to go through life and walk somewhat of a straight line, God and I would get along fine.

After several day's of exhaustive searching, I went to the Courthouse in downtown Lawton to see if their was a job I could do, or at least apply for. As I entered the Courthouse, I noticed a large bulletin board with several sheets of paper hung by tacks. My eyes were fixed upon what appeared to be an application for a license of some kind, which as I read further, I found it was a license to be a Process Server.

Figuring out that I could probably do that type of work, I went to the Court Clerks office to inquire. The woman at the desk told me I could obtain a license to serve Legal papers and in addition, start my own business. She explained all the steps necessary to get started.

I was curious as to how much money I could make, moreover, who my clients might be. The clerk told me I could charge about twenty dollars or more per paper served, which she explained, would be up to me. She said that my main clients would be attorney's. Gathering the paper work I needed, I filled out the application, and if my background check was favorable, the Judge would sign it.

I left the Courthouse in good spirit's knowing that after a five-day waiting period, I could be in business. Driving the downtown area that same day, I noticed several Attorney's offices, which I hoped, would someday be clients of mine.

Arriving back home I told Tracy of my plans, which he was excited about, mainly because I would be bringing in an income. However, I had the waiting period this as I remember, seemed an eternity. Meanwhile I continued to help around the house, which kept me in good graces with the family.

After completing the five-day, wait period, I went to the Courthouse to check on my application, which if it was signed, I could start soliciting clients. I really needed to work for myself, as I did not like having a boss scrutinizing my every move.

Arriving at the Court Clerks office, Mary, the woman who had help me with the application process, greeted me with a smile and said, "Your license is ready". I was jazzed and something made me feel Mary was looking out for me, almost hoping I would be successful in my endeavor. She explained that if I needed any help to call her, as legal papers can be hard to interpret.

The next morning, I stopped at all the finance companies and several Attorneys' offices. Enthusiasm filled the blood in my veins as I put in a hard day of looking for work, however with no real leads. Disappointed, I knew tomorrow was a new day.

As I was talking with perspective clients, I realized this would not be easy. Most places I checked told me they already had a Process Server, and some would not even take my business card, which cost me a fortune to have printed. Frustrated, I thought I might have to take a job, any job, while my business was being built. It looked as though my over confidence was starting to wear me down, as if I became unable to accomplish my goals. I began thinking that maybe I should not have left Oregon, this was a depressed area and the people seemed somehow different.

More and more, money was becoming the issue and I was getting desperate. I had very little money left in the bank and had to do something fast. I realized that if I were to stay in Oklahoma, my business would have to support me and I was going to have to work hard.

That next morning, I was feeling defeated mentally and physically. The weather was blustery and cold, as I drove back into Lawton to canvass the Attorney's offices once again, and suddenly it happened. While speaking with a secretary at an office I had not yet been to, I started to give my sales pitch when the secretary interrupted and said, "Most of the Attorney's in this area use Don Scott"; "You might speak with him about a job". From the information she gave me, Mr. Scott had a large operation that for the most part, handled all of the Legal Process for the state. I was excited, thinking I could finally get my foot in the door. With the directions to Mr. Scott's office in hand, I went to speak with him immediately.

As I entered the two story downtown office, I noticed several suites within the building. Don Scott's office was first on the right, as I walked in feeling a little timid. Sitting at a desk in the reception area, was a nice looking woman that appeared to be in her thirties, typing diligently as she looked up and smiled, "Can I help you", she asked. My voice was low as I asked to speak with Don Scott,

"Just a moment" she said, "What is your name?" she asked.

"Jason" I said.

The office looked small as I scanned the area while she went to get Mr. Scott. I felt weird being there, as I might have been his competition if things had worked out.

"Tell him to come in" a voice from a nearby office said.

Brenda the secretary, told me to go in Don's office and he would be with me shortly. I could not help but notice Brenda's pleasant demeanor and her professionalism, which was a comforting feeling.

Entering Mr. Scott's office, I felt nervous as he asked me to sit down. Behind this large desk sat a small thin man, with glasses, and graying hair. He had the most unorganized desk I had ever seen. But who was I to judge, as he asked, "What can I do for you"? For some reason, I could hardly remember my own name as I stuttered while introducing myself.

"My name is Jason, and was wondering if you were looking for a Process Server"?

"Was that your license on the board at the Courthouse?" he asked.

"Yes" I said. Don then asked if I had any experience in this type of work,

"No" I said, "However I am a hard worker and a fast learner". Don then wanted me to tell him a little about myself, and if I was from this area. I explained to Don that I was from Nevada originally, but most recent, from Oregon. I went on to say that, I got out of the Military at Ft. Sill in August of 1989, which seemed to get his attention when he found that I had been in the service.

Don began to show me some pictures of him, when he was in the Army, explaining that he was a retired officer. I looked at several pictures of helicopters, as he told me he was a pilot, while in the Army.

We seemed to hit it off well as I thought he knew I was a clean-cut individual, also well dressed and motivated. Don and I spoke for an hour or so when he asked if I would go with him to the Courthouse,

"Sure" I said, thinking to myself that he may hire me.

Driving home that day, feeling as though I was on my way to a bright future, I could not wait to tell Tracy of my good fortune. Don had asked me to start at eight thirty the next morning.

One thing that caught my eye as I spoke with Don was that he was a sharp dresser, and very well educated. I knew I had to come in to work ready to learn the business.

The next morning I awoke early and was ready for my first day on the job. I arrived at the office at eight-thirty well motivated wearing slacks, pressed shirt, and tie, and still looked under dressed compared to Don.

After several days of intense training, I was out on my own, mainly because Don was short handed, and he felt I was ready to do the job. I worked in town for a few weeks and found it difficult to find addresses, most of this was lack of familiarity with the area. I did manage to serve a high volume of papers in a short time, which impressed Don.

I started going out of town working long hours, and was hardly ever home. My car was on the road six and seven day's a week, racking up high mileage and constant engine trouble.

By the end of the first month on the job, I had been in every small town in the southwestern portion of the state. People were always so friendly, that I could locate just about anyone. Information in the smaller communities was easy to come by, however their were times when folks would not tell or give information, which made it difficult to find someone. Since I was out of town often, Don had installed a cellular phone in my vehicle to keep in contact with the office.

For all the hours I put in, I felt I was not compensated very well, and was often tired but still happy that I was employed.

Three months later, around June, Don put me on a salary and gave me a monthly vehicle expense, which was a big help to my pocket book. At that, particular time in my life I rarely called friends and family back home.

Although I liked my job, I soon learned things were not always perfect. If I made a mistake on a paper Don would get upset, even if it were not my fault, as he was very particular about the way his employees did their jobs. Incompetence was unacceptable. Don had a quick temper and a short memory, but everything considered one of the most generous and caring individuals, I had ever met. I remember on several occasions Don would hand me fifty dollars out of his pocket almost knowing I needed the money, and would never take it out of my pay.

By the time July rolled around, the summer heat was almost unbearable to work, not to mention live. I was loaded with papers and I told Don we would need more help. Business was booming as I could hardly keep pace with my current workload. We had other people working, however, they were only part-time, and this made it difficult for me.

Near the end of July, I was making enough money to get a place of my own which would allow me to be closer to work.

The next morning I began looking at the classified ads and found what I thought would be perfect, and I called to get directions to a house in the Lawton area. I spoke with a woman, Rosemary, who explained that she had a room in her house for rent, and asked if I would like to see it. I told her I would be there to look at it right away.

As I pulled up to the house I noticed the area looked rundown, but the house looked nice. Walking up to the front door, I was pondering whether or not I would feel comfortable living in someone's private home. Just before I knocked on the door, a woman stepped out and asked if I was the person that called for the room, I told her I was. I asked her if she was Rosemary, which she replied "Yes", with a heavy German accent, and then invited me in the house.

The house on the inside looked new, and quite cozy, not to mention spotless. My immediate thought was that this was the place for me.

Rosemary was a short elderly woman with gray hair, and an accent that was hard to understand. She explained everything about the place and wanted to know if I had a job, and could pay the monthly rent. Once I told her where I worked and how long I had been on the job, Rosemary agreed to let me move in that day. By the time, night fell, I was already moved in, almost like a member of the family.

A month went by and I was living comfortably in my new place, with the exception of an annoying roommate that had just moved in. Her name was Carrie, and she always seemed to have conflicts in her life, moreover let everyone know about them. I was not home much so it never bothered me, however Rosemary did not like listening to Carrie's problems. Rosemary and I got along fine and I always enjoyed talking with her, especially since I had no friends.

I was working long hours all through the summer and had little time for extra curricular activities, or anything else. It seemed as though I was living to work, not working to live, however my life was about to change, forever.

TWO

After several months of working with very little help in the office, Don had hired Eric Smith, a shy, soft spoken young man to help with the ever increasing work-load. Eric, who was well-built, tall, and had dark brown hair did a great job for the office. We became good friends as well as co-workers. I was glad to have the extra help.

While at the office one day in late November 1997, Eric asked, "Would you like to go with me to my friend's house this weekend?"

After a brief pause, "Sure" I said, "a two day break from work would be great." I was pondering why Eric would want me, to go, and not go by himself.

"Jason, do you believe in ghosts?" Eric asked.

Laughing, I said "No! Why? Do you know any ghosts?" I asked jokingly.

"Jason, don't laugh, this is a serious question." I knew he was serious by his stern look.

"Eric, spirits do not exist." I said. "There is no proof that I know of which say's they do exist."

"Jason, what if I told you they do exist?" Eric asked. "I have seen strange things happen at my friend's house."

"Eric, is this the friends house you want to take me to this weekend?"

"Yes" Eric said smiling.

"So, are you telling me the house we are going to is haunted?"

"Yes" he said, as his face began to turn red. Jason, let me tell you what I know, because I have experienced many strange occurrences at this house."

Eric explained that he had a friend, who took him to this house in the small town of Centrahoma, Oklahoma. "I first went to this house in 1995, he said. Maxine and her husband Bill Mcwethy own the house. I have been there several times in the past two years mostly on weekends. Every time Maxine's daughter Twyla showed up at the house while I was there, strange things would happen."

Eric explained that, "Twyla did not live with Maxine, she and her husband Steve Eller, along with their two children Megan and Desiree, lived near Oklahoma City about two hours north of Maxine's house.

"What kind of things would happen?" I asked Eric.

"Well." he said, "I would be sitting at the kitchen table talking with Maxine and Twyla, when suddenly out of nowhere I would be hit with an object. I have been hit with rocks, coins, silverware, glassware and other items including eggs. Many times I have run out of the house so scared, I did not want to go back."

"I spent the night there one time, and while I was sleeping, I was awakened by the sound of something hitting the wall above my head. I jumped out of bed and noticed that my hair was covered with something wet. I turned on the light and found an empty bottle of shampoo on the floor. The reason that I want you to go with me is because I am afraid to go alone. Also, I would like to see if you might find a way to prove that this is all a hoax." If Eric was trying to uncover a hoax, maybe he thought that two sets of eyes were better than one.

"Eric, I will go with you however, you will never convince me ghosts are real."

I left the office that day puzzled by what Eric had said. I did not believe in spirits, or haunting, but I decided to keep an open mind about what Eric had told me. I could not help but notice the way he looked at me while he told me about this house. It was as though he was preaching to me, and trying to convince me that what he was telling me was true.

We left for Maxine's Friday evening November 28th, around six o'clock. I was thinking to myself that nothing was going to happen at this house. If something did happen, I felt certain it could easily be explained. We took my car but I let Eric drive since I did not know how to get there. As we were driving to Maxine's house I asked Eric, "Do you think anything will happen at Maxine's tonight?"

"Maybe, he said, but don't expect anything to happen since you are a new person to the house. I have been at Maxine's house when a new person visited, and nothing happened. People have come from all over the state to visit this house and many went away disappointed, because they did not experience anything."

We were only about twenty miles from Maxine's house, when Eric told me about two of the spirits that were supposedly at the house. "Michael," he said, "is a playful spirit. He will whistle when he wants you to know he is there. He also throws coins and eggs at anyone in the house."

"Leader, however, would get more violent. He would throw dishes, silverware, and rocks to try and hurt someone. Sometimes we cannot tell if Michael or Leader, would cause the disturbances.

"How do you know the names of these spirits?" I asked Eric.

"Maxine told me she has talked to both Michael, and Leader." Eric explained. "The spirits told Maxine who they were."

"Jason, we are getting ready to cross Leader Creek Bridge. Every time I cross this bridge I get chills. Once we cross Leader Creek Bridge, we are only about five miles from Maxine's."

"Eric, do you think Leader Creek Bridge, and Leader the spirit are connected in anyway?"

"I don't know" he said, looking puzzled.

Suddenly I asked, "Eric, did you say Michael whistles when he wants you to know he is there?" A chill ran down my back.

"Yes. Why?"

"Well I just heard three soft, short whistles, right next to my head."

Eric chuckled. "Yeah right Jason."

"I am not kidding!" I told Eric.

Eric nodded his head, "All right, we might get some serious action tonight." I could tell Eric was excited by the way he perked up when I told him I had heard a whistle.

Eric pulled off the highway into the small town of Centrahoma. With an intense look in his eyes, Eric asked, "Are you ready for this Jason?"

"Ready for what?"

"You will see" Eric said, with a grin.

Even though it was dark, I could tell the town was small. "What is the population here?"

With a smirk Eric replied, "Damn small, about 100 people."

We then pulled in to this narrow driveway off of a dark street. I saw a bright porch light that was almost blinding to the eyes. With an excited look Eric said, "We are here."

The first thing I noticed as I stepped out of the car was the house looked small. In the movies, haunted houses were much larger by comparison. My immediate thoughts were, this is a hoax and nothing was going to happen as far as spirits and ghosts were concerned.

As Eric and I walked up to the porch, I could see that the house sat on a large lot. I saw one large shed behind the house and one smaller shed to the right of the driveway. The porch light was bright enough for me to see a cluster of trees at the back right corner of the property.

Just as we were about to knock on the front door, the door opened, and a middle-aged woman said, "Hi Eric, is this your friend?"

Eric nodded, "Maxine, this is Jason."

"Hi Jason how are you?" Maxine inquired.

"Fine," I said with a friendly smile.

"Well, come on in," Maxine said.

Maxine was a short, thin woman with a nice comforting demeanor. I could tell she was quite friendly as she greeted us. Maxine looked to be in her early fifties.

Walking into the house through the kitchen, I saw an older man sitting at the kitchen table. "My name is Bill, Maxine's husband" the man said, as he stood to shake my hand. Bill looked to be about the same age as Maxine.

"Hi I'm Jason, thank you for allowing me to visit this weekend."

Bill was tall and thin, and seemed friendly but reserved.

I started gazing around the kitchen area and noticed the walls were tattered with stains.

Maxine saw what I was looking at and said laughing, "The walls are a mess from Michael throwing eggs at everyone." "I just made a pot of coffee. Would you like some Jason?"

"Sure." I could not help but notice how hospitable Maxine was, as she handed me a cup of coffee.

Also sitting in the kitchen was a young girl who looked about twelve years old. Maxine explained that Heather, the young girl, was her granddaughter.

Maxine said, "Heather's mother Kim was at home just up the street."

Heather was tall, thin and had long blonde hair. At first, Heather was very shy, but opened up while we talked.

As Maxine invited everyone to sit at the kitchen table, she asked, "Jason, did Eric tell you about the strange things that happen at this house?"

Pulling up a chair, I hesitated and told her, "Yes, but I just don't believe in spirits or ghosts."

"I want to show you some photographs of items that have been thrown at us." Maxine said. She pulled out a photo album full of pictures she had taken at the house. She showed me a picture that was taken right after a handful of what appeared to be small crushed rocks, which she said, had fallen out of the ceiling directly onto the center of the kitchen table.

'The rocks," Maxine explained "fell out of the kitchen ceiling as Twyla and I sat at the table one night. I was so scared when that happened."

Pointing to another picture, she said, "Here is a picture of the living room wall after Michael threw an egg at us but missed and hit the wall. And this picture here is of a box with silverware, coins, rocks, and other things that Michael had thrown at us."

Maxine then showed me some newspaper articles that were written about her house. As I read through the articles I realized that Maxine's house had been the center of local and statewide media coverage concerning spirits and haunting.

"Many people have visited my house in the hopes of getting a frightening experience. I think that is how the media found out about my house."

I stood up from the chair and stretched my legs; I felt cramped from the car ride over to Maxine's. I excused myself and walked into the living room. As I looked around, I could not believe how torn up the walls were. Stains of all sizes were located on every wall in the room. I could not help but wonder if these walls had ever been painted. I peered into the hallway and saw three small bedrooms and a bathroom off the living room.

I felt embarrassed, but I asked anyway, "Maxine, have you ever painted the inside of this house?"

"No, I'm afraid to," she said, "Michael will just tear it up again."

In the living room were a sofa, a loveseat, and a Lazy Boy recliner. The living room was medium size. There was also an entertainment center with a television.

I asked Maxine if I could use the restroom, which she replied, "Yes, it is in the hallway." When I walked into the bathroom I felt a chill come over me, as though I was nervous to be in a closed room alone in this house. Being a skeptic I should not have felt this way.

When I left the restroom, I went to join the others in the kitchen. As we were talking, a car pulled into the driveway. Through the kitchen window, I saw a woman, and two young children get out of the vehicle and head toward the house.

Eric shouted, "Twyla's here!" Eric jumped up from his chair and ran out to greet Twyla. In just a minute, Eric walked back into the house with a young woman and two small girls. The older of the two girls looked to be around ten years of age while the youngest looked about four, or five. He introduced me to Twyla, who seemed to be very friendly. Twyla was short, had a medium build, and shoulder length dark hair. Twyla appeared to be in her mid twenties. Twyla had the most angelic face I had ever seen. Eric also introduced me to Twyla's daughters Desiree and Megan. Desiree was tall, thin, and had long dark hair. Meagan, the youngest, was short with red hair.

We all sat down in the living room. Except for Bill who went to his bedroom. Bill did not seem to enjoy all the company and the house was loud with everyone talking. From his facial expressions, I felt some tension in the air. Bill's demeanor changed when Twyla came to the house. He would not stay in the same room with Twyla. I wondered what he thought about what went on at the house.

"Is Steve coming over later?" Eric asked Twyla.

"Yes, right after band practice." Twyla laughed, "Every time Steve stays the night here, Michael throws shampoo and eggs at him while he tries to sleep."

"Twyla, why do these strange things only happen when you're around?" I asked her.

"I don't know they just do."

"Who is Michael?" I asked Twyla.

"I think he is a little boy." Twyla explained. "When Michael laughs, he sounds like a small child."

Sitting on the couch, looking toward the kitchen entryway, my eye caught an object coming right at me. A penny hit me in the cheek just below my left eye, and I jumped off the couch.

"Oh shit!" I shouted. The penny seemed to come at me from the direction of the refrigerator. I immediately ran to the kitchen to see if anyone was there.

My heart was racing as Eric shouted, "It's starting!" I looked around the kitchen and found no one there. I quickly returned to the living room. I thought to myself, everyone that was in the house was sitting in the living room with me, with the exception of Bill, who was in his room. I suppose the penny could have been thrown from someone in the living room. I started to watch everyone closely just to make sure I could account for there whereabouts. I got excited, but remained skeptical. Something big would have to happen to make me think otherwise.

Looking surprised, Twyla said, "I can't believe something would happen this fast on your first night Jason."

Maxine went into the kitchen for some coffee and yelled out, "I hear something in the refrigerator!"... Splat! I turned around as an egg hit the wall right next to where I was standing. My heart jumped as I ran back into the kitchen with everyone right behind me. Everyone in the house was frightened as we gathered at the kitchen table.

The egg came within inches from hitting me. It happened so fast I did not notice where the egg came from. My breathing was rapid as I tried to figure out what was going on. The egg could not have come from the direction of the kitchen where Maxine heard a noise in the refrigerator, because it would have had to bounce off two walls to land where I was standing.

Moments later, we all sat back down at the kitchen table wondering what would happen next. We talked for about fifteen minutes. Eric kept looking over his shoulder while we talked. I could tell by the way he was looking around; he was waiting for something else to happen.

With a bored look Eric asked, "Twyla, do you want to go to the cemetery?"

"Yeah" if you and Jason want to go."

"Will something happen at the cemetery?" I asked Twyla.

"I don't know," she said. "Sometimes when we drive through the cemetery Michael will throw things inside the car."

Her eyes were wide with excitement as Maxine said, "We can take my car."

"I don't want to take the kid's to the cemetery" Twyla said with a nervous tone in her voice. The two girls, Desiree and Megan were begging to go with us. Twyla reluctantly said, "Okay, just this one time."

As I climbed into the back seat with Eric, Megan, and Desiree, I noticed a bottle of Coke partially consumed in the back window. I was thinking, luckily the cap was on, since it was lying on its side. Twyla and Heather jumped in the front seat and Maxine would drive.

"I heard a whistle!" Maxine said laughing. "Oh we are going to have fun tonight."

It was a quick drive to the cemetery. Everyone in the car was talking about their experiences with spirits so the mood was set as we pulled into the front gate. Tall bushy trees lined each side of the road creating a bearer between the road and the cemetery. Occasionally there would be just enough of a gap to catch a glimpse of the tomb-stones permanently resting in the quiet surroundings. If it had not been for the headlights of the car, we wouldn't have been able to see the cemetery at all.

We were all having a good time, laughing and joking about Michael and Leader, and trying to scare each other with the creepy surroundings. Just as I was getting into the moment, we heard a very loud "CRACK!" followed by a ringing sound. I thought a rock, or something metal had just hit the window. Hard!

"What was that?" I asked.

"Oh my god!" You could hear her voice quiver as Twyla shouted, "Michael threw this quarter at my window and it landed in my lap!" I looked over at the window where Twyla had been sitting, expecting it to be cracked or broken because of the impact; it was not. Eric tried to huddle closer to the middle of the back seat. Shaking with fear, Desiree and Meagan moved over towards me. We were all trying to stay away from the car windows.

Fascinated by what had just happened, we were encouraged to continue driving through the cemetery. "Oh shit!" Eric shouted, "I am totally wet!" Eric was reaching over his shoulder, feeling his back. As he looked over towards me, I suddenly felt something wet on the back of my neck and shoulders. "It's on me too!" I said. Since the girls were between Eric and me, I asked Desiree and Meagan if they got wet. After checking themselves, they replied no.

I cried out, "How the hell did that happen?"

Looking around for an explanation, Eric said he felt something next to his feet as he reached down on the floorboard in the back seat, and picked up a plastic coke bottle. It was the same Coke bottle I saw earlier, but now the cap was missing.

27

"Oh lord!" Maxine muttered, "That's Heather's Coke from yesterday; she left it in the back window of my car when we came home from the store."

Eric sniffed his hands and said he could smell the Coke.

Worrying about the kids, Twyla suggested we should go back to the house. Twyla could see by their expressions, Meagan and Desiree were scared. Heather and Maxine were stunned by what had happened.

I told Eric, as we were driving back to Maxine's, "I remember seeing that coke bottle in the back window as we got in the car to go to the cemetery. The coke bottle was about half full with the cap appearing to be secured on the bottle."

I was getting a weird feeling because I could not figure out how that cap came off that bottle. I did not see Eric, or the two girls reach for anything in the back window.

It was almost midnight as we pulled into Maxine's driveway. Twyla told the girls they would have to get ready for bed. I was the first to get out of the car. Eric and everyone else went in the house.

I started walking toward my car so I could get a paper towel out of my car cleaning supplies box, where I stored my Windex, Armor all, rags, etc. I needed to wipe the soda off my neck and shoulders. I still had no idea how the soda spilled all over Eric and me.

Suddenly I felt butterflies in my stomach. As I approached my car I noticed some writing on the roof of the car. I was taller than the height of the car so I could see it easily.

I walked up slowly to the passenger door... "Son of bitch!" I said, shocked by what I was looking at. My home telephone number was written on the roof of my car. I could see it clearly as it was written over the dew on the roof. I took a few steps back and gathered my thoughts.

First of all I thought, Eric has never known my home phone number, as it was listed under my landlords name in the phone book. The only number Eric has ever reached me at was my cell phone number. Second, I had just met all of these people and they did not know my number either. Even my boss, Don, did not know what my home phone number was.

I rushed back into the house and asked everyone to come outside. I said with a demanding voice, "I have something to show everybody!" Eric was the first one to my car.

"Somebody wrote a number on the top of your car Jason?" Eric asked.

"Who could have known my home number?" I asked. I looked at Eric to see his reaction, he seemed nervous. "I don't remember seeing that on my car when we left to the cemetery." Maxine, Twyla and Heather looked confused as they starred at the writing on my car.

"Jason," Eric said, "I swear I do not know your number, so I could not have written that on your car."

As my voice jumped in pitch, I told Eric, "I did not imply that you wrote this on my car.

I started thinking that many things were happening which I could not explain.

"Let's go back in the house." Maxine said.

"I've got to get those kids in to bed." Twyla said, as she took her girls back inside.

"Are you and Jason staying the night Eric?" Maxine asked. "We will if you don't mind" Eric answered. "I would enjoy the company." Maxine replied.

Eric told me we would sleep in the living room. Twyla made a bed on the floor in the living room for her and the girls. Maxine, Twyla, Eric and I all sat back down at the kitchen table. Desiree and Megan were laying on the floor in the living room.

"What time will your husband be here?" I asked Twyla.

"Not until about three in the morning."

Rubbing his hands together and smiling, Eric said, "That is when the shit is really going to fly."

As I was sitting at the table, I continued to look at the articles that Maxine showed me earlier in the evening. Eric was sitting to my right, Maxine to my left, and Twyla was sitting across from me...Bam! I jumped from the table, as some rocks fell from the ceiling above onto the kitchen table.

"Oh god! Oh god!" I said. It was like a bomb had exploded as everyone stumbled over each other to get out of the kitchen. "This could not happen; rocks do not fall out of thin air!" I said in a frightened voice.

The rocks fell directly onto the center of the table. Eric looked pale white and wanted to leave the house and go back home. After we retreated to the living room, I waited a few minutes and then went back into the kitchen. I thought for sure I would find a large hole in the ceiling but there was no hole to be found. I was mystified. I was looking at a perfectly good ceiling, and a pile of small to medium size jagged edged rocks on the kitchen table.

Everyone decided it would be better to sit in the living room together. I could see that the children were scared when we ran out of the kitchen. The two girls cuddled next to Twyla.

"Maxine, has anyone ever been seriously hurt by the things that have happened here?" I asked curiously.

"About two years ago, I don't know which spirit it was, but someone pinched my breast so hard it started to bleed."

"Thank god I don't have breasts!" I joked. Maxine started laughing; I could tell she had a great sense of humor.

That night, as I got to know Maxine, Twyla and the kids, I started to feel what would become a long relationship developing.

"Have you ever had a paranormal investigation done on your house Maxine?" I asked.

"Yes" she said, "A production company came and stayed seventy two hours. They stayed in a motorhome outside while monitoring the inside of our house using sound and video equipment. They would not let us have the kids at the house while they did their investigation because they didn't want any interference from the noise of the kids. They said they found some strange activity, but would not tell us anything about what they found."

"I will get you guys some blankets and pillows." Maxine said. "I have to go to bed. When Steve comes home it could get crazy around here and I might have to get out of bed."

"I'm tired too." Twyla said. Maxine told Eric and me we could sleep on the two couches. Twyla and Steve would sleep down on the floor with the two girls.

In between the two couches were a small table and lamp. I noticed that the lamp was the only light source that I could see in the living room. Eric and I rolled out some blankets on the couches, shut the light off and tried to get some sleep.

My sleep was interrupted by the sound of a door opening. I sat up on the couch and turned the lamp on. This large man walked in to the living room and said,"You must be Jason."

"Yes. Are you Steve?"

"Yes, how are you doing?"

"Fine" I said yawning.

"Has anything happened tonight?" Steve asked.

"Oh yeah." I said smiling.

"I am going to get some sleep." Steve said, "We will talk in the morning."

"Goodnight." I said.

I tossed and turned and could not sleep. Steve was snoring so loud, it sounded like a freight train coming through the living room when suddenly his snoring stopped… "Damit Michael!" I heard Steve say. Twyla woke up, "What's wrong Steve?" she asked.

"My hair is wet! Michael threw something on me." Twyla turned on the lamp. "Shit, it's toothpaste all over my hair!" Steve said, as Twyla started laughing.

"Here is the tube of toothpaste." Twyla said, as she picked it up off the floor.

Steve went to get a towel to clean the toothpaste out of his hair…Smack! I heard jumping from the couch looking at an egg dripping from the wall behind the recliner. I looked over at Eric, who was just waking up, probably from all of the noise we were making.

"That was one hell of a hard thrown-egg!" I said to Twyla. Frightened, I went to the kitchen to get a paper towel and clean the egg off the wall. I could feel my heart pounding. Steve came back in from the bathroom and tried to lie down and get some sleep. I helped clean the egg off the wall and then sat back down on the couch.

"We are not going to get much sleep tonight." Steve said angrily.

Twyla turned the light off and we all went back to bed...Dink! Dink! What sounded to me like metal objects, were being hurled around the living room. I refused to get up and turn the light on. Everyone except me was asleep. I was getting scared so I tried to wake Eric. He was sleeping heavily. I shut my eyes hoping it would just go away, and eventually it did. I finally got to sleep as the sun was rising the next morning.

November 29th, Saturday morning, I was awakened by Maxine's voice telling everyone that breakfast was ready. I caught the smell of fried potatoes cooking.

"Did you sleep well Jason?" Maxine asked as she set some plates on the table

"For about two hours. You didn't hear all that noise last night Maxine?"

"No, I slept like a baby."

"Someone was throwing something in the living room last night. Steve had a tube of toothpaste squeezed in his hair." I said laughing. "I tried to wake you up Eric."

"I did not hear a thing." Eric said.

"Have some eggs and potatoes Jason." Maxine said.

It was about nine-thirty when we sat down to eat breakfast. While we were eating, we talked about the things that happened the night before. At one point, making jokes about Michael, and Leader. I asked Maxine if it was Michael, or Leader who caused the disturbances the night before. "I think it was Michael because he likes to throw things and keep everyone from sleeping. Leader does not visit much, and I'm glad because he is violent."

"Is there a Wal-Mart or K-mart anywhere near here?" I asked.

"Ada has a Wal-mart." Twyla said.

"Eric would you like to run in to town with me?" I casually asked.

"Sure" he said.

"I want to pick up a video camera." I told him.

"You can try a video camera Jason, but I don't think it will work here." Maxine said.

"Maybe it will." I told Maxine. "I also have a 35mm camera with me so I can take some pictures."

At around eleven o'clock, we left for Ada, which was about twenty miles away, to go to Wal-mart. I didn't tell anyone, but at the time, my intentions for buying a video camera were solely for the purpose of catching a member of Maxine's family creating what I still believed was a hoax. As we drove through the small town of Centrahoma, which I had not seen because we arrived at night, I noticed it was very small. A light scattering of houses and mobile homes, with a quaint little country store, made up the tiny community, located on the north side of highway 3, in south eastern Oklahoma.

Two hours later Eric and I returned to Maxine's with some video equipment I had purchased from Wal-mart. I started to unload the video camera from my car and set it up in the kitchen area. Eric and I did not to use the battery pack, but instead, we plugged the camera into an outlet.

I set the tripod in place and mounted the camera on the tripod. I made sure to set up the video camera in the far left corner of the kitchen. The camera sat in the corner where two walls met. I wanted to make sure I could view the entire kitchen and not allow anyone to get behind the camera, without being seen on tape. Maxine commented that the location of the camera was a good idea.

Eric and Maxine were the only people in the house with the exception of Bill, who was sleeping in the back bedroom. Twyla, Steve, and the kid's had left for a short time.

With the video camera in place and plugged in I went out to the car to get the blank video-cassettes, for recording. When I came back into the house I was stopped dead in my tracks as I entered the kitchen.

"What the hell!" I shouted. Covering the lens of the video camera was a saltine cracker. As I got closer I noticed nothing was holding the cracker over the lens. Maxine and Eric ran into the kitchen.

"What's wrong?" Eric asked me with a nervous expression on his face.

"Somebody put this cracker over the lens of the camera." I said in an angry tone of voice.

I grabbed my 35mm camera and took a picture of the video camera with the cracker over the lens. I started to pull the cracker off the lens and became enraged with what I saw. The cracker had been held in place by a pat butter which I thought was from a container that was open on the counter.

The first thing that came to mind was this camera is ruined. Maxine and Eric could see that I was upset with what had happened.

I sat down at the kitchen table and starred with disbelief at the lens of the video camera. The butter that held the cracker in place was all over the rubber lens shield that went around the lens. I went over to the counter to inspect the tub of butter that was sitting with the cover off. I could tell the cracker had been dipped into the butter.

I looked at Maxine and Eric and realized by their expressions, they had nothing to do with what happened to the video camera. I was not away from them for more than twenty seconds.

Eric and I started to clean off the lens so we could continue to use the camera. While I was cleaning the camera, I began reflecting on the last fifteen hours spent at Maxine's house.

When all of the strange things occurred in the house, everyone was accounted for. Even the Coke bottle incident in the car at the cemetery had no reasonable explanation. I would have seen someone throw the eggs and coins in the house, because I watched everyone closely. If this was all a hoax, it was the best illusions and acting I had ever seen!

At two o'clock that afternoon, we finished cleaning the camera lens, and a nap sounded good since I was completely exhausted from lack of sleep the previous night. I thought it would be a good idea before I went to sleep to put a new cassette tape in the video camera and start recording. I also set the focus control on manual.

I woke up after only an hour of sleep that afternoon. Twyla and her family returned around four o'clock. I told Twyla what had happened while they were away from the house. Twyla reacted cautiously as she tried to understand what happened to the video camera.

"I'm sorry about your camera Jason." she said, with a look of sympathy. "Nothing strange has happened in at least two weeks until you came here."

I started wondering if maybe there might be some past history with Maxine's house that could explain why these bizarre things were happening.

I asked Maxine if anything had happened here with the previous owners of this house. "If anything happened at this house, we were not told about it when we bought the place."

"Maxine, how long have these strange occurrences been going on?" I asked.

"The first strange events occurred on the evening of, June 15th, 1990. One night while my family and I were sitting outside on some chairs, we were suddenly attacked with rocks. Rocks were hitting the house with great force."

While Maxine was explaining to me about when the strange activity began I checked the video camera to see if anything was on the tape. The camera had been on for about an hour. The main thing I was looking for on the tape was a family member staging a hoax.

I walked up to the video camera and could see that the power had been turned off. I turned the power back on. I could clearly see the tape inside the cassette holder. As I looked at the cassette I noticed that only a small portion of tape was used. I wondered why the video camera would shut off when just a small amount of tape was recorded. I knew that if Maxine or someone else had played with the video camera it would show on the tape, someone approaching the camera.

After rewinding the tape, I pushed play and watched the viewer on the camera. I watched as the camera recorded Maxine sitting at the kitchen table. The camera was focusing in and out rapidly, as if someone was rotating the lens. I did not see Maxine or anyone approach the camera during the recording. Suddenly the tape shut off and the screen went blank. I looked at the auto/manual focus switch and found it was still on manual focus. I was shocked and confused. I knew enough about video camera's to know that auto focus activates with motion. Manuel focus does not activate with motion of any kind.

I read the manual over and over and came to the same conclusion: I could not explain what happened with the recording or the malfunction of the focus on the video camera. I put a new tape in and continued to record for the rest of that day. I would wait until I got home to watch the tape that was currently recording.

Maxine made a big chicken dinner for everyone that Saturday evening. After dinner Steve and Twyla left to go to Steve's band practice. Bill had dinner with us and went to bed shortly after dark.

Maxine, Eric, and I, along with Twyla's two daughters, sat around the kitchen table and talked most of that night. I remember drinking a large amount of coffee, thinking I would not get any sleep when Twyla and Steve came home. Nothing had happened during the time Twyla and Steve were gone. The house seemed eerily silent.

At around midnight I went to sleep. Maxine and Eric also went to bed.

I woke up Sunday morning about eight-thirty. I must have been exhausted. Everyone was eating breakfast. I felt somewhat disappointed that I went through the entire night without something being thrown at me. Still I had a memorable weekend at Maxine's with everything that I had experienced, and knew I would return. I enjoyed being part of the strange things that went on at her house.

I loaded my overnight bag and video equipment in the car and at eleven that morning, I said goodbye to Maxine, Twyla, Bill, Steve and the kids. Eric and I left to go back home.

We were excited by what we had experienced. I mentioned to Eric on the way home that I wanted to go back to Maxine's again. Eric told me we could go back the following weekend.

THREE

The winter cold was beginning to set in as I contemplated my next trip to Maxine's house. The excitement started to build when Eric mentioned during our drive back from Maxine's that we would be returning to the house of supposed spirits the following weekend. I had a lot to think about that Sunday, however, I needed to get some work done. During all of the excitement the past two day's, I almost forgot I had a job.

At five o'clock that Sunday evening, I went out to serve some papers and try to get caught up from not working that weekend. I worked until about ten o'clock, and then went home.

The first thing I did when I got home from working was talk with my landlord, Rosemary about the weekend I spent at Maxine's. Rosemary and I were comfortable enough to talk to each other about anything. She was also a wonderful person to allow me to share her home.

We sat and talked for about an hour. I told her everything that had happened at the house I had visited.

As I told Rosemary about the strange happenings at the house, I could see her eyes begin to open wide, and her face express an interest in what I was saying.

A story that is this bizarre would cause the average person to express disbelief, but not Rosemary; she was very attentive to what I had experienced. I told Rosemary I did not believe any of this could happen without an explanation. I also explained that I did not believe in any of the spirits that Maxine claimed, inhabited her home. Eric, too, had a hard time believing any of this was true.

As far as I was concerned, everything strange that happened at Maxine's had been circumstantial, and had not been proven to me, to be authentic. While telling this story to Rosemary, I found myself wanting to go back to Maxine's house. I wanted to return to the house to see if anything else would happen, and perhaps to expose a fabrication, and close this part of my life.

I went to my room around eleven o'clock after talking with Rosemary. Rosemary went to bed. I wanted to look at the video-tape I recorded Friday and Saturday. I watched the recording from start to finish. Once again, I could see the focus during the recording being manipulated in some way. The camera was focusing in and out. I did not see anyone approach the video camera at anytime during the recording. Then I set up the video recorder in my room to do a test recording. I wanted to see if the same malfunction of the video camera would happen at my house.

I put in a new cassette tape; put the focus on manual, and started to record my room. Then I took a shower, and returned about ten minutes later.

I watched the video I had just recorded. I could see no malfunction with the recording. Everything recorded was clear, and the focus on the camera worked fine. The camera did not focus in and out.

I looked at the clock, as I got ready for bed. It was eleven-thirty. As I lied down on my bed, the phone in my room rang. It startled me because I was not expecting a call from anyone that late in the evening. I looked at the caller ID on the phone as it rang; it displayed "caller unknown." I picked up the phone. "Hello, " I answered.

In a voice that sounded like a small child, I heard, "Hi Jason, this is Michael."

"Hi." I said, thinking I did not know anyone named Michael.

"Are you coming to Maxine's this weekend?" the voice asked.

"I hope so," I said.

"I love you Jason, bye."

I stayed on the line as the voice faded out. I did not here the caller hang up the phone. During the brief conversation, the background noise in the phone sounded hollow as we spoke to each other.

When I hung up the phone, I felt a cold sensation come over me. The fact that the names Michael, and Maxine, were mentioned during the phone conversation gave me chills. Just then, I had a thought, maybe someone in Maxines family wrote down my phone number the night it was written on top of my car. Then suddenly I realized this would be difficult to prove.

I knew I would see Eric at work the next morning, and I would mention the phone call to him then. I wanted to call Maxine after I got off the phone, but I did not have her phone number.

I thought that someone was trying to scare me by saying the caller was Michael, Maxine's spirit, and that was the reason for the phone call. If someone was trying to trick, or frighten me, it worked.

I woke the next morning and got ready to go to work. I could not wait to ask Eric, if he knew if a member of Maxine's family called me last night. Eric could have set this phone call up with Maxine, as a hoax. I thought that if Maxine or someone in her family called me, they would let me know it was just a joke. Maxine and her family seemed genuinely honest. I also knew Eric well enough to know, he would not play a trick like that, just to scare someone.

When I arrived at the office that morning, I saw Eric getting out of his car. I walked up and told him about the phone call I had received the previous night. I asked if I could get Maxine's phone number. He gave me the number and I mentioned that I would call her after work. Eric told me it was probably one of the kids in Maxine's family that called my house. He told me it was definitely was not him.

I called Maxine about six o'clock that Monday evening. I explained to her about the phone call, and the contents of the conversation. Maxine's response was that Michael may have called my house. Actually, she was convinced it was Michael who called. She told me the phone call could not have been made from her house. Maxine explained that she had a long distance block on her telephone, and could only make local calls. Since I lived three hours away, my number would have been long distance.

I casually asked Maxine if Twyla or anyone else in the family could have called my house. Maxine stated, "She did not know of any reason why they would call me. No member of my family has your phone number."

"Maxine, do you mind if I come over this weekend?" I asked her.

"No," she said, "I wouldn't mind at all."

"Eric will come with me I'm sure."

"That's great, we will have fun." Maxine said excitedly.

"I hope Twyla can come over," I said.

"When she calls me, I will ask her to come down to my house on Friday night."

Before hanging up the phone, I said to Maxine, "we will see you on Friday evening."

Thinking back to the strange phone call that night, the voice sounded very distinct. I did not recognize the caller to be anyone I had met at Maxine's. This particular voice was squeaky, and high pitched, and would have been difficult for someone to disguise.

Eric and I talked frequently that week about the two nights we spent at Maxine's. We even joked around, about the spirits that supposedly haunted the house. Eric mentioned that he could not wait to go back to Maxine's house.

Friday, December 5th, arrived and we were ready to leave for Maxine's. We left that evening at five o'clock. Eric and I made sure to bring the video camera.

At eight-thirty, Friday evening, we pulled into Maxine's driveway. Maxine came out to greet us as we walked up to the front porch of the house.

"Hi Jason, how are you doing? Eric, how are you?"

"Fine Maxine, thanks for letting us come back to your house," I said, as we walked through the front door.

Maxine smiled, "Are you sure you guy's can handle another two nights at this house?"

"Oh yeah, let's have some fun," Eric responded.

"How are you Bill?" I asked, as he was sitting at the kitchen table.

"Good, nice to see you again."

Eric and I sat down at the table with Maxine, and Bill.

"Let's have some coffee Jason, because you're not going to get much sleep tonight if you stay here," Maxine said with a smirk.

"Maxine, I know you told me that a production company came out to do an investigation; has your story appeared on any other television broadcasts?"

"They told our story on the news show 20/20 in 1996."

"Did anyone around the state visit your house after the broadcast?"

"Oh you bet, but people were coming even before our story was on television."

Bill stayed and talked with Maxine, Eric and me, for about an hour. He then excused himself and went to watch some television in his bedroom. According to Maxine, Bill enjoyed watching westerns, which I said I too, like westerns, especially the ones with John Wayne.

Twyla, Megan, and Desiree arrived at the house around nine-thirty that evening. We sat all at the kitchen table and talked. Steve had gone to Tupelo, four miles north of Maxine's, for band practice.

As Twyla, Maxine, Eric, and I talked, Twyla and I seemed to connect well, as far as our personalities were concerned. We were able to laugh at one anothers jokes and comments. I enjoyed her wonderful sense of humor. Eric, and Twyla, also got along well I noticed. Out of all the people I had met in my lifetime, Maxine, Twyla, and the rest of their family, made me feel the most comfortable.

At about eleven o'clock I asked Twyla and Eric if they wanted to drive to the cemetery. Twyla agreed to go, but without the kids. She seemed apprehensive about involving her two young children in all of the strange things that went on around the house, and at the cemetery. I noticed the previous weekend that Twyla became frightened on several occasions while she was in the house. Eric was aching to go to the cemetery, even though he admitted being scared.

Maxine stayed at the house with Desiree and Megan, while Eric, Twyla, and I went to the cemetery.

We walked out to my car, a 1993 ford escort, and two-door hatchback. My car was not fancy in any way. Everything was manual, including the door locks, and windows. My car was small inside. The back seat separated the two front seats and hatchback area. The hatchback compartment contained a heavy plastic Locktite box. Inside the box were all my cleaning supplies for washing the car. A heavy plastic lid covered the box. Two handles on the sides of the box locked the cover in place.

Eric jumped in the back seat, Twyla got in the front passenger seat, and I drove. Eric positioned himself in the middle of the back seat, so he could hold the video recorder and video tape the ride to the cemetery.

We pulled out of the driveway and turned right onto First Street. Moments later Eric, while pointing the video recorder toward the front seat, complained that he could smell an odd fragrance within the car. Just then, Twyla said she felt something wet on the back of her neck. I asked Eric if he had the video on record. He explained he was recording and at the same time, looking through the viewer screen. I could see through the rearview mirror, both of Eric's hands were gripped tightly around the video camera. I could also see the red power light, glowing in the darkness of the car.

Suddenly, I heard a dull THUMP! THUMP! sound coming from the back seat. I stopped the car in the middle of the road, and everyone jumped out of the car. Eric was still carrying the video camera.

"What was that Eric?" I asked.

"I don't know," he whispered.

I felt something dripping off the side of my neck. I wiped my neck with my hand and could smell Armor-All, a cleaning solution I used for my car. Twyla, while running her hands through her hair, said she could smell Windex, which she explained was sprayed into her hair. Eric and Twyla stood away from the car near the side of the road.

I walked around to the rear of the vehicle to see if someone was hiding in the hatchback area. I stayed about two feet away from the car as I looked into the vehicle, through the windows. My stomach felt overcome with butterflies. I started to get nervous. I glanced at Twyla, and Eric; their eyes were wide with wonder.

"Oh my God," I muttered.

"What do you see Jason?" Twyla asked in a stuttering tone.

"The cover is completely off my cleaning supplies box."

I peered through the back window and was shocked that my Armor-All, and Windex bottles, were both missing from the box. I could easily see inside the box from outside the vehicle. Even though it was dark outside, a street lamp close by illuminated the area.

Eric, did you spray us with my cleaning bottles?" I asked him.

"No" Eric replied, "I was holding the video camera the whole time."

"I saw him holding that camera Jason, I even looked back at him while we were talking," Twyla explained.

Twyla gave me a look as though she thought I did not believe her, or Eric.

I walked to the driver's side of the car, and looked down through the side window. I could hear my heart pounding as I looked on the floorboard behind the driver's seat; there I saw a bottle of Armor-all, which lay on its side. My eyes then focused on the back seat behind the front passenger seat. There on the seat, lay a bottle of Windex. I asked myself, how could Eric not have noticed that Windex bottle lying next to him?

During my inspection of the car, Twyla, and Eric, remained about five feet back from the passenger side of the vehicle. Eric still had the video recorder with him, but he was not recording. Eric was holding the camera down to his side.

Twyla shouted, "Let's go back home!"

I opened the driver's car door, pulled the front seat forward toward the steering wheel, and picked the bottle of Armor-All up off the floor. I then reached further onto the back seat and grabbed the Windex bottle.

After securing the two bottles of cleaning solutions, I opened up the hatchback. Still frightened by what had happened, I quickly returned the cleaning bottles to the Locktite box. I covered and locked the lid down, and shut the hatchback on the car.

"Twyla it's okay; let's get back into the car, and go to the cemetery," I told her.

Eric was also nervous about going to the cemetery. Twyla reluctantly agreed to continue driving to the cemetery.

We entered the car and drove further down the road. My thoughts were confused, and I was in total disbelief, as to who could have sprayed us with the Armor all, and Windex. Twyla kept repeating that we should not go to the cemetery, because she had a bad feeling inside, but I was excited and her pleading didn't really register with me. Eric was reluctant, but said we should keep going.

Eric, sitting in the middle of the back seat, began recording once again. I kept looking back at him just in case he was responsible for spraying us with the cleaning solutions. I also watched to see if he would try something else, if in fact, it was him who was causing things to happen.

Suddenly, I felt a cold wind inside the car, followed by a white powdery substance filling the cab of the car. As I tried to wipe the powder off my shirt with one hand, with my peripheral vision, I saw my prescription glasses moving from my right side, hovering in thin air, at eye level, and then appear in front of my face. It felt as though time had stood still, everything was in slow motion. Before my eyes, my glasses were squashed in from the sides, and dropped onto the floorboard between my feet.

I looked back at Eric; he was covered with white powder. Twyla, as I looked at her, was also covered with powder. They were both trying to wipe the powder off themselves.

Reacting on pure adrenalin, I hit the brakes, put the car in park, opened the door, and yelled "Everyone, Get out!" as I jumped out of the car. Twyla and Eric quickly got out of the car and ran to my side of the vehicle.

"Please tell me you got that on video Eric," I said, hoping he did.

"Where did all the powder come from?" Eric asked.

"I don't know, but it did not come from my car," I said.

Twyla asked, "Are you okay?" "What happened?"

My eyes must have looked as big as golf balls, as I asked Twyla, "Did you see what happened to my glasses?"

She replied, "No," as she gave me a strange look.

"Eric, did you see anything from where you were sitting?" I asked.

"I didn't see anything," Eric replied. "Maybe we got something on video," he said, with a hopeful expression.

The car door was still open as I approached the driver's side. I reached down onto the floorboard of the driver' seat, picked up my glasses, and showed them to both Eric, and Twyla.

The glasses looked crushed beyond repair. The right lens was missing. Twyla turned a shade of white as she looked at my glasses. Eric could not believe what he was seeing. Eric then tried to video-tape the glasses still in my hands, but the video camera would not turn on. Every time Eric would push record on the camera, the power would automatically shut off. I looked at the video camera and could see that the battery power indicator was showing a full battery.

I carefully put the crushed glasses in the glove box. I then told Eric to make sure that the video camera was working properly.

"I have to find the other lens; I can't afford a new pair of glasses," I told them, in a state of panic.

I turned on the inside compartment light, and started looking for my lens. I searched the entire vehicle and could not find the missing lens. Eric and Twyla also helped in the search.

We were all perplexed.

"Jason, this is getting bad," Eric said nervously.

Everything happened in such a short amount of time; I looked back toward Maxine's, and realized we were only a block away from her house. We got back into the car and continued to drive towards the cemetery. I had to see what would happen when we got to the cemetery; I could not turn back now. Everyone got back into the car.

Twyla was scared but I, on the other hand, was angry by this point. Eric just sat quietly. He kept looking over his shoulder hoping nothing would happen to him. Once again, he sat in the middle of the back seat, and started to record with the video camera facing toward the front of the car. Eric said that the camera seemed to be working again. The only thing I could think about was the fact that I would have to buy new glasses, which I could not afford. I needed my glasses for work, because I had to locate addresses in the dark.

We turned through the front gate of the cemetery. Twyla made one last plea for us to return to Maxine's house. I begged Twyla, "Please, let's just drive through the cemetery one time, and then we will go back to the house."

Nodding her head yes, Twyla relented, and we started making the circular drive through the cemetery.

About halfway through the cemetery, I started hearing a CLICK! CLICK! Sound. Twyla kept looking over at me, as though she had also heard the noise.

"Eric, do you hear that clicking noise?" I asked him.

"Yes, I think it's you're door locks," he said, as his voice quivered.

"Jason, stop pushing your door locks up and down!" Twyla shouted.

"I hear something in the back seat with me," Eric muttered.

"Twyla, I have both hands on the steering wheel, how can I move the door locks?

I could see Eric in the rearview mirror, and he wasn't moving a muscle. Eric's hands continued to clutch the video camera, which he held at eye level, recording as we drove.

The noise continued, coming from inside the car, I looked to my left and saw my door lock moving up and down all by itself; I nervously wondered what was happening.

"Twyla, I don't have automatic door locks."

"Jason let's go!" Twyla yelled.

Suddenly Eric screamed out, "The hatchback just opened!"

I could feel cold air entering the car as I looked through the rearview mirror. My hatchback door was moving up and down as we traveled on the bumpy dirt road of the cemetery.

"Let's go back to the house NOW! Jason," Eric yelled.

I sped up the car and started toward the exit. Moments later, I heard a loud THUMP, coming from Twyla's side of the car. It came from outside the car.

"We just hit something Jason, pull over," Twyla said in a frightened voice.

"I'm not pulling over; we're getting the hell out of here!" I yelled to Twyla.

I drove faster than I had ever driven, to get back to Maxine's house. We pulled into the driveway at the house, and everyone jumped out of the car. I ran to the rear of the car and shut the hatchback. We ran toward the front door. Just then, I felt a sharp pain on my lower right leg. I also heard what sounded like a rock, or something, hit the side of the house. I kept running; I was not about to look back and see what had hit the house.

"I just got hit with something Twyla," I said, as we scrambled to get inside the house.

We almost forgot to open the front door, as we ran inside. Out of breath more from the events we had just witnessed than from running, we explained to Maxine what had happened after we left the house. Once inside the house, I pulled up my pant leg and did not find any marks where I felt the pain.

Twyla was clearly upset when she told Maxine about my glasses, and she seemed sympathetic to the fact that I would have to buy a new pair. I showed Maxine the damage done to my glasses.

Eric looked pale, when he said, "I'm not going back to the cemetery anymore."

"Oh my Lord Jason. I am so sorry," Maxine said, looking sympathetic.

"Jason, ask Michael to give you your lens back" Maxine said.

"This is nuts Maxine," I exclaimed. "I don't want to ask Michael for anything!"

I looked at the clock and realized we had only been gone from the house for twenty minutes. I asked Eric to come out with me and look at the passenger side of my car, just in case I had hit something on the road while at the cemetery.

We walked out to the car and looked at the outside of the passenger door. I did not immediately notice anything that could have caused the loud thump. Upon inspecting the door more closely, my eye caught a glimpse of a small hand print; I could see it quite well, due to the dust on the car and the bright light from Maxine's porch.

"Eric, come look at this."

As we looked carefully at the hand print, I could see only a three finger impression in the dust on the car. Eric and I both inspected the entire side of the car to see if any dents or scratches were visible. I thought that a rock might have been ejected from the tire while we were driving. We found no dents or scratches. I was definitely sure I heard a thump on the outside of the car, near where Twyla was sitting. Twyla also heard the thump.

Eric and I went back into the house to see if anything had been recorded on the video camera during our trip to the cemetery. We re-wound the tape and looked at the recording through the view-finder. I was shocked to see that the camera had somehow shutoff at the point before the white powder appeared. Eric, I thought, may not have noticed the camera was off. The only recording on the tape was when we first got in the car to leave to the cemetery. The camera had just shut off. Eric and I were disappointed.

Back inside the house, I saw Twyla getting the kids ready for bed. Even though it was late, I was not tired. Twyla made a bed on the floor for herself and the girls. Maxine went to one of the bedrooms to get Eric and me some blankets and pillows. I could tell by looking at Twyla that she was exhausted. Maxine handed us some bedding and told everyone goodnight. I made my bed on the couch closest to the kitchen. Eric would sleep on the recliner. After we settled in for some sleep, I reached over and turned off the lamp.

Nervous about falling asleep, I kept one eye open and both ears on alert. Not five minutes later I heard something hit the living room wall next to the television.

"Stop it Michael!" Twyla hollered out, "I'm tired and want to sleep."

"Yeah, stop it" Megan repeated. The house became silent as everyone except me, drifted off to sleep.

A rustling noise in the kitchen made me sit up on the couch. "Twyla," I whispered, "someone is in the kitchen." Twyla did not respond. By the sound of her breathing, I could tell she was sleeping heavily. Everyone else in the house was also sleeping. I thought to myself, this is just great! I keep hearing noises, and these people are sleeping like bears in hibernation.

I got off the couch and reluctantly went to the kitchen hoping to find some coffee still warm in the coffee pot. Before I got to the kitchen, a light came on. It was Steve; he had come back from band practice.

"Did I scare you?" Steve asked.

"After what we went through tonight, yeah, you did," I told him.

I then told Steve what had happened.

"I could see why you were startled when I walked in the house."

Steve walked into the living room and sat down on the floor next to Twyla, and the girls. He said he was tired and ready for bed as he laid his head on the pillow. I set up the video recorder in the kitchen, exactly the same way as I had previously done. I went to bed hoping for a quiet night of sleep.

I must have slept hard. The next morning I awoke to the sound of people talking in the kitchen. I looked at the time; it was eleven in the morning. Eric was still sleeping.

"Whoa, I really slept last night," I told Maxine, as I sat down at the kitchen table with a cup of coffee.

"Maxine, can I hook the video camera to your television, so we can see if anything was recorded on the tape from last night? I started recording just before I went to sleep."

"Sure" she said, "Maybe we will see Michael on there."

"Wouldn't that be nice? I said, laughing.

Eric was just waking up, as I was connecting the video camera to the television. I pushed rewind on the camera and it just clicked. I thought to myself, this tape wont re-wind. I pulled the cassette tape out and found that the tape did not record.

"Maxine, I can't get this camera to function properly at your house."

"That's okay Jason; that production company that came to my house could not get their video equipment to work properly either."

57

I explained to Maxine that I had tested this video recorder at my house, and it worked fine. I then took the video camera back into the kitchen, and decided to try again. I asked Eric if he could check the instruction manual to see if everything was set properly on the camera. He said it looked right to him.

Steve finally got out of bed about twelve o'clock. He walked into the kitchen, and at that point we were all sitting around the table. Maxine said she had to use the bathroom, and left the room. Twyla started to tell Steve about the things that happened the night before when suddenly, Maxine yelled out.

"Michael wrote something on the mirror in here!"

I jumped up from the table and picked up my 35mm camera. Entering the bathroom I saw the letter"M" written on the mirror. As I looked down into the sink I saw a tube of white toothpaste, missing its cap, lying in the sink. I could still see toothpaste oozing from the top of the tube. I was puzzled by what I was looking at, and noticed everyone else just starring at the mirror.

I took a picture of the mirror and then touched the "M" with my finger. I smelled toothpaste on my finger. It looked like the same toothpaste that was lying in the sink.

We all walked back to the kitchen and sat down. Nobody seemed surprised at what we had found. I gathered quickly that Maxine was use to things happening, and did not seem concerned. According to Maxine, she had seen this type of writing before.

I got up from my chair and walked over to the coffee pot. As I was pouring my coffee I noticed a pan on the stove. The pan was filled with leftover chicken scraps from the previous night's dinner. I noticed the pan also had what looked to be, grease, or oil inside. The pan looked to be about a two-quart size.

I poured my coffee and started back to the table… From behind my back I heard a loud CRACK! Followed by something metal that had been dropped onto the kitchen floor. I looked down at my feet, and saw that my shoes were covered with the contents of the pan that had been on the stove. The pan had struck inside the door jam of the kitchen entryway. Everyone freaked out and ran to the living room.

"That was meant for me Maxine," I said.

At that moment I thought, if whatever this is can throw a pan filled with left over food, it could damn sure throw something sharp, like a knife. From that moment on, I started looking over my shoulder, hoping to have a little more reaction time.

I went back to the kitchen a few seconds later to help clean up the mess. Chicken scraps in used cooking oil was everywhere on the floor. I took a towel and wiped off my shoes. I noticed the walls were covered with the liquid from the pan. The force of the pan hitting the wall caused the liquid to splash in several different directions. We spent the next thirty minutes cleaning the walls, and the floor in the kitchen.

Eric, Maxine, and I, spent the rest of that afternoon looking at Maxine's property. Behind her house stood a long rectangle building in bad need of repair. The building had a small garage, with an attached living area. The living area at one time was used for a bedroom. One of Maxine's daughters's occupied the room some years earlier, she explained. As I entered the tattered living quarters I felt a cold presence. Maxine followed closely behind as we went further into the building.

"Okay, I'm ready to look at the rest of the property," I told Maxine. I did not feel comfortable in that room. The room was filled with furniture, mattresses, and other odds and ends. Nails were scattered all over the floor. The room was dusty and looked like it had not been lived in for quite some time. Maxine mentioned that one time there had been some activity from one of the spirits in the room. She had heard something hitting the wall, followed by nails being thrown in her direction.

Eric said as we were walking around the property, "I don't like that room next to the garage; it gives me chills."

We left that building and went further into the back yard. Maxine showed me a concrete cellar located in the back left corner of the property. I wrestled the door open, and looked down the steps into the cellar. I could see some old bottles sitting on a shelf inside. The cellar was small, maybe 8x8 feet in size.

"We will have to come out here at night," she said. "Michael has thrown some rocks and coins at us when we tried to come out here after dark."

"I don't think I want to enter this cellar," I said, as I stood at the door peering in.

Even though it was mid-afternoon, I could sense something was not right about the cellar. As we walked away from the cellar, I noticed some fruit trees in the right corner of her property.

"Are those apple trees?" I asked.

"Yes they are, Michael has thrown apples at us on several occasions," Maxine replied. "We would all sit outside during the hot evenings, and apples would fly out of the trees in our direction."

Maxine, Eric, and I started back to the house. Maxine wanted to fix an early dinner and try to get some sleep.

After we finished eating, Steve had to get ready for work. As a police officer, he often worked twelve-hour shifts; he had to drive back to Wileetka that evening to be on time for patrol.

Bill watched some television for about two hours, and then went to bed. It was around eight o'clock that evening when Eric, Twyla, Maxine, Desiree, Megan, and I went to the kitchen and sat down at the table. We talked Maxine into staying awake for a little while longer.

Maxine asked Twyla to pick a year, and write that on a piece of paper, but not show, or tell anyone the date she chose. After writing the date, Twyla layed the paper face down on the center of the table.

"Now Jason, Maxine said, you wait for a few moments, and a coin will be thrown at us with the date that Twyla wrote on the paper." I said sarcastically, and under my breath, "Here comes the magic tricks."

We all continued talking when suddenly; a coin flew right past my head and hit the window next to where Twyla was sitting. I could hear the whistling sound of the coin fly right by me, leaving me startled. The coin landed on the window seal. Twyla retrieved the coin and looked at the date...

"Oh god, I did not think it would work," Twyla said, with a surprised expression on her face.

She turned the paper over that was on the center of the table, and revealed the date she had wrote. I looked at the date on the paper, and looked at the date on the coin. "Unbelievable," was the only word I could come up with, to describe what had just taken place. Twyla had written the date 1988, on the paper. Maxine explained that Twyla had once before, been able to request a coin with the year that she asked for. Eric was shocked, and in awe of what Twyla had done.

"Why 1988," I asked Twyla.

"That was the year Desiree was born." Twyla said.

We had all just witnessed what could only be construed as, one hell of a magic trick, if that were indeed the case.

Maxine stood up from her chair and told everyone goodnight. We were all exhausted, and I thought that this was a good time to go to bed. We had to leave early that Sunday morning and go back to work Sunday evening.

I told everyone good night and that Eric and I would be leaving around eight in the morning.

"Maxine, Twyla, thank you for having us over this weekend, I'm quite certain I will be back soon if you folks don't mind."

"Jason, you and Eric, can come and stay whenever you like. We would love to have you here," Maxine said.

I slept right through the night and awoke refreshed. If something had happened while I slept, I would have never known, as I was mentally and physically exhausted. Eric was awake and ready to go back to Lawton.

We loaded the car at seven-thirty Sunday morning, as Maxine was sitting at the kitchen table. We told her goodbye, and asked her to tell everyone who was still sleeping, we would see them again, soon.

While Eric and I were driving away from the town of Centrahoma, I felt as though I was leaving my own family. These people would make anyone feel welcome, like a family member. While driving home, I could not help but feel that nothing had been resolved. I had neither exposed any kind of hoax, nor could I explain anything that happened.

We were about thirty miles from home when I realized I had not taken any pictures of the events that took place at Maxine's. Eric told me he did not even think about taking any pictures. I was thinking that in the heat of the moment, and in my haste to figure out how the things that happened could be explained, I had overlooked taking any photographs. The strange events had unfolded so quickly that I had no time to react, or think about anything else. There was no doubt in my mind that Eric and I were now treading in unfamiliar waters.

FOUR

While thinking about Maxine's house and what was happening there, my mind suddenly reverted back, to when I was a young adult. I remembered watching the television show, Unsolved Mysteries. I would watch the people on the show tell stories about their house being haunted, or that they had seen a ghost. Back then, I laughed at those people, thinking how ridiculous their story sounded. Now, after I had spent some time at Maxine's, questions began to come to mind: How many people throughout the world, have claimed to have witnessed a haunting? Were these people of sound mind, or were they "A sandwich short of a picnic?" Were these average, everyday, hard working, and blue-collar people? Were these people wealthy? And more importantly, were these people religious? Did they, themselves, believe in ghosts? I then had to ask myself, what kind of a person was I, before I had ever gone to Maxine's house.

I fell into the average, everyday, hard working, and blue-collar category. I knew nothing about ghosts and spirits, before I had ever gone to Maxine's house; I had never personally witnessed a haunting. I belonged to no religious denomination, but I knew I believed in God. One thing that I was adamant about was this: I did not believe in ghosts.

When I got to work Monday morning, Eric was already in the office. The first words out of his mouth upon seeing me enter the office were, "I cannot believe what happened to us this weekend. Jason, I don't think I want to go back to Maxine's for awhile."

"Eric, I have to go back, please come with me."

"Maybe we will go this next weekend Jason, but after that, I don't want to go back for awhile."

Eric and I went our separate ways that morning. Before leaving the office parking area that morning, I opened the hatchback of my car and looked everywhere for my lens. I carefully removed everything in my locktite box, so I could inspect the inside. I checked the area around the locktite box. I checked under my seats, in the glove compartment, and on the floorboards, but I could not find the lens.

After working a few hours, I found it very hard to concentrate on my job. My curiosity about what was going on at Maxine's house was occupying my mind. I was no expert in the field ghost hunting, and I didn't even know if such a specialty existed, but I needed to find some information about that particular subject.

I was not the type of person you would find at the library; but that was the only place I knew that might have what I was looking for. That afternoon I went to the local library.

When I told the clerk standing behind the counter at the library what I was looking for, I got a strange look. I was embarrassed, wondering what she thought of me. Nevertheless, I was determined to find out what Maxine might be dealing with on a daily basis. The librarian pointed me to the section on ghosts.

I thumbed through several books on the subjects of ghosts, spirits, and haunting; I was struck by the number of books wriiten about these subjects: Just in the ghost category, there were around 75 books. I found there are several different types reported. A ghost could be the living spirit of one's soul, after they had died. A ghost may or may not appear as an apparition. If a ghost appears as an apparition, it is usually seen in a pale shadowy form. A ghost could be a demon. There are ghost ships, those ships, which had disappeared under strange circumstances which were never explained. An example would be: The lost ships of the Bermuda triangle. Several witnesses reported seeing those lost ships appear within the Bermuda triangle, from out of nowhere, only to disappear moments later. After reading about ghosts, I was sure of one thing I did not see any apparitions at Maxine's house. Someone or something, was throwing things around the house, but it was not your typical ghost.

Spirits, were the next subject on my list: Spirits could haunt, possess, or inhabit a home, property, or a certain area. They could be good or evil. A spirit could be an angel, or demon. One type of spirit is called, an Incubus: An evil male spirit thought to have descended upon and had sexual intercourse with a sleeping woman. Another type of spirit would be, a Succubus: A female demon supposed to descend upon a sleeping male and have sexual intercourse with him.

While looking through some other books on the subject, I kept coming across the word "poltergeist." I found a book on that subject and began reading. A poltergeist manifests itself by making noises, rapping sounds, or creating disturbances. Poltergeists have been known to move objects around in many different ways, such as: Making an object disappear from one place, and reappear in another place, usually reappearing in a certain area that had no real significance to the place it was moved from. An example of this would be: An object that has been moved from a table in the kitchen of a house, and being place in a car, or in the yard outside of the house. Poltergeists have also been documented as being able to move large furniture across a room. Poltergeists can also throw things; mainly small objects like rocks. One theory exists that tells of poltergeists using a living person, most often a female under the age of twenty, as an "Agent" that allows the poltergeist to manifest itself. The "Agent" or living person may have repressed anger, and hostility and most commonly, sexual tension. I also read that it is uncommon for a poltergeist to inhabit a person for longer than a year.

One would think that after reading that poltergeist's could move things around, a light would come on in my head. I had been hit with small objects like pennies, quarters, small rocks, and eggs, not to mention witnessing my glasses hover in mid air and then crushed before my very eyes. I did not want to believe that a poltergeist was haunting Maxine's house or family. The very word poltergeist scared the hell out of me. The hair on my neck stands on end, when

I think that a poltergeist could throw things at you at anytime, from out of nowhere. Even though I had this information about poltergeists, I still refused to believe, and dismissed the idea of poltergeists as so much nonsense.

Most of the books that covered these subjects offered a lot of insight into the world of haunting. I read many stories about people who had witnessed being in the presence of demonic ghosts, and spirits. These people claimed to have been scratched, and had their hair pulled, which caused them mental and physical anguish.

After spending several hours, reading about these subjects, the thought that one of these ghosts, or spirits inhabiting Maxine's house still sounded ridiculous. I kept asking myself the same question: If it's not a haunting causing these bizarre things to happen, then what could cause the strange incidences? What significance does the supposed ghost, or spirit, have in relation to Maxine, Twyla, and her family? I would probably never be able to answer that question. But I would try to, again, and again, and again.

Even though I felt I was somewhat better educated on the supposed haunting at Maxine's house, I was no closer to understanding what was happening there. I realized that I was becoming engrossed in Maxine's house; I felt as though I wanted to be there all the time. I wanted to find out for myself, who or what was responsible, for the crazy disturbances at her house. At this point, I did not feel like working at all.

I finished working that Monday around five o'clock. I thought I should go home and make some phone calls to my family and friends back in Oregon.

The first call was to my mother. I told her about the experiences I had the two previous weekends. I was not surprised to hear her tell me that I needed to see a psychiatrist. My mom said she thought someone in Maxine's family was creating a hoax. I explained to her that I watched everyone closely, but I did not see anyone in Maxine's family do anything out of the ordinary. When the strange incidences occurred, everyone was accounted for. My mother wanted to know if I was going to move back to Oregon. I told her that I did miss the ocean, and all my friends back home. I told her, I would most likely move back to Oregon someday.

After talking with my mother, I called some friends, and they wanted me to move back home, too. I was starting to think that maybe it was time to move back to the West Coast. I thought I might need a change of scenery. The only drawback was, I was really getting to like Maxine and her family. So I called Eric and asked if he would go with me back to Maxine's. Eric agreed to go one last time.

The next three days, before returning to Maxine's were nerve racking. I could not think about anything else but going back to her house. I felt as though I was being pulled into a vortex of the unknown. Work was no longer a priority; it had now become an inconvenience.

Thursday morning, the day before Eric and I were to return to Maxine's, I was driving around serving papers. I suddenly felt the urge to ask for my lens back. "Michael, would you please allow me to find my lens?" I asked, though I had no idea that I would get a response. That evening when I got home, I looked once again in the hatchback area of my car. Sitting right beside my locktite box on the carpet of the hatchback, I found what I so badly needed, my lens. Remembering what Maxine said, "Just tell Michael you need your lens," I had to step back and count to ten. I suddenly was overcome by chills.

I called Maxine and told her the good news. Maxine could not believe I found my lens, as she thought it was lost forever. Maxine explained to me that Michael would take money and other items from her, which, were never to be seen again. I told Maxine I could not wait to come back to her house.

The next morning I rushed with my lens and the crumpled glasses to the eye clinic, where they were repaired. The person who repaired the glasses asked how this happened; I told him I had sat on them. I could not tell him the truth; I was too embarrassed.

Eric and I left Friday night December 12th, at seven o'clock, heading back to Maxine's house. This time we took Eric's car. Eric was excited about going.

We got to the house around ten-thirty that evening. Much to our dismay, Maxine told us that Twyla would not be here until later that night. Maxine and Bill were the only two at the house. Although I was disappointed that Twyla would not be there until later, it was good opportunity to see if something strange would occur without Twyla present.

Suddenly, I realized I had forgotten to bring my video camera. Eric said he thought that would be okay, because we had such a hard time getting the camera to work properly the last two weekends.

Maxine made a pot of coffee and we sat around the kitchen table talking, mainly about the prior weekend. I told Maxine that I was glad we could take the time off work. Eric and I always worked weekends because we were so busy. I was beginning to think less and less about my job.

Maxine told us that Bill was not feeling well and had gone to lay down, but that she would stay up with Eric and me for awhile.

"I'm glad you will be staying up with us Maxine, I sure enjoy you're company," I told her as we were drinking our coffee.

We had talked about thirty minutes when the conversation started to lag.

"Eric, let's drive to the cemetery," I said.

"Boy, Jason, you're just asking for trouble," Maxine said, with a big grin.

"I can't help it Maxine, although I'm scared at times when I am here, my curiosity calls out to me. Would you like to go with us Maxine?"

"No, that's okay, you guys go, and I'll stay here."

"Okay, let's go," Eric said excitedly.

When we got down to the cemetery the gate was closed.

"The gate was not closed last Friday, Eric."

I could see the scared look on Eric's face. His hands were shaking. After what had happened last Friday, I could understand why he was so uneasy.

"I don't feel right about this Jason; let's go back to Maxine's," Eric said nervously.

"It's an omen Jason, the cemetery does not want us to drive through here tonight."

We drove back to Maxine's and she told us she was going to bed. She said she was tired and not feeling to well. Maxine brought out some blankets and pillows. Just then, Twyla and her two girls walked in the front door.

"Hi Twyla, how are you doing?" I asked.

"Fine. I didn't think you two would come back after last weekend."

"We couldn't wait to come back," I told her.

"I just dropped Steve off at band practice; he will probably stay there all night," she said.

Twyla went to the back bedroom to get some bedding for her and the girls. She told us she wanted to get the kids in bed early. After making up her bed on the floor in the living room, Twyla stayed up for about thirty minutes, and then went to bed.

Eric and I were not tired, so we stayed awake and drank coffee. The house was eerily quiet as we sat at the kitchen table talking. I told Eric that I had gone to the library to find some information on ghosts and haunting. I told him everything I had read on the subject. Eric seemed happy that I wanted to find out what was happening at Maxine's.

"Eric, I can't figure out why this spirit, if it is real, would attach itself to Twyla."

"I think it's because she is a mother with two children, and Michael is also a child," Eric said.

"Do you really think Michael looks to Twyla as a mother figure?" I asked Eric.

"If this is real Jason, I would say anything is possible."

Eric and I had many questions, but no answers as we struggled to understand what we were dealing with at Maxine's. We were amateurs who were ignorant of the world of ghosts and haunting. Eric and I were determined to find the answers we were looking for, if there were any to be found.

Twyla and her kids had been in bed for about an hour, when we decided to get some sleep. I made my bed on the Lazy Boy recliner. Eric wanted to sleep on the couch. The time was twelve-thirty, when we shut the lights off and tried to get some rest.

I just layed there for about two hours; I could not sleep. "Eric, are you awake?" I whispered.

"Yeah, I'm awake. I can't sleep," he whispered back. We were trying to be quiet so we would not wake Twyla and the girls.

STOMP! STOMP! STOMP! STOMP! STOMP! STOMP! I heard next to me on the floor, as I bolted upright on the recliner.

"What the hell is that?" Eric said, in a loud voice.

"I heard about six or eight stomps. It sounds like someone is running through the house!" I yelled to Eric.

We were both sitting straight up on our beds, when suddenly we heard the kitchen door open.

"I sure hope that's Steve," I said.

The stomping became louder as the noise came from the kitchen and continued through the house. I got out of the chair and ran over to Eric. The sound of the stomping increased as the floor beneath my feet was vibrating.

"Eric, I don't see anyone!" I yelled, as my heart started to palpitate. I peered into the kitchen and saw the door to the outside was wide open. Without any hesitation, I quickly ran into the kitchen and shut the door. I then hurried back to the living room to wake Twyla..

"Wake up Twyla," I said shaking, as the sweat dripped from my forehead.

"Turn the light on Jason!" Eric hollered out, as he was getting off of the couch.

I ran to the lamp that was on the table between the two couches, and turned the light on.

"Eric, someone is running through the house, but I can't see anyone."

Then, as suddenly as it started, the stomping had quit. The house went silent. Eric's face was pale white.

"Eric, I don't know what is happening, but I am not going to stay here if I have to listen to that stomping all night."

"I don't hear anything now," Eric muttered, as he sat back down on the couch.

Eric and I tried to wake Twyla, but she was sleeping soundly. I got back on the recliner and tried to go back to sleep. I was nervous and my hands were still shaking from all that stomping. Eric reached over and turned the light off…

STOMP! STOMP! STOMP! The stomping started again only moments after we got settled. Eric jumped off the couch, as the stomping continued.

"We are getting the hell out of here!" Eric said emphatically. Eric then turned on the light.

"Twyla, Twyla, wake up!" Eric shouted.

"What's wrong?" she asked, as she awoke from her slumber.

"Jason and I heard the kitchen door open, and someone stomping through the house."

"I'm not staying here tonight," Eric told Twyla.

"I didn't hear anything," Twyla exclaimed.

"We tried to wake you, but you were sound asleep," I said to Twyla.

"Get your things together Jason we're leaving."

Eric was really upset; his face pale white, as if he feared for his life. I could no longer handle the stomping noise. I grabbed my bag with my clothes, and we told Twyla, good-bye.

Eric and I headed for the kitchen door to leave the house. I opened the door and just as I stepped onto the outside porch, I was struck in the forehead with a small rock that fell at my feet. I didn't stop to pick it up. I felt my chest tighten as I started to run towards Eric's car. Eric was already opening his car door when I shouted that I had been hit by a rock. Eric jumped in the car, started the engine, and almost left without me. The car was already moving when I opened the door and jumped inside. Eric peeled out of the driveway. I looked at his face, and he appeared withdrawn almost as if he wasn't conscious to what was happening. After being run out of the house and hit with a rock I realized, if I had never known fear before, I knew it now.

The time was about four-thirty Saturday morning. We had been on the road for about twenty minutes before Eric was finally able to speak.

"Jason, I am not going back to Maxine's; I have never been run out of her house before."

"Eric, what is going on at that house?"

"I don't know, and right now I don't really care, but I'm not going back there again."

The ride home was silent at times, as we drove through the small towns that dotted the southeastern part of Oklahoma. While driving home Eric mentioned that he could feel a cold presence in the car. I did not feel scared anymore, but I was very anxious to find out more about what we were dealing with at Maxine's house. I began to feel like I was driven by some unknown force which I was not familiar with, that was sucking me into the perplexing mystery.

"Eric, sometime in the near future, I need to go back to Maxine's."

"Are you crazy," he said, with a surprised look. "If you go back to Maxine's house, you will have to go without me."

Once again the car became silent. I slept off and on during the ride home. Exhaustion had finally taken over my body. We arrived back home around eight o'clock that Saturday morning. Eric dropped me off at my house, and I told him I would see him at work.

I slept the entire day, waking at around six in the evening. I went out to serve some papers, but the excitement I had felt about my job in the past, was gone. I had a new focus on life, and it wasn't work related.

A month had past since Eric and I were run out of Maxine's house. We occasionally talked about our experience there, but Eric was reluctant to speak about that night in detail. We were busy as ever at work, and Eric was thinking about quitting his job. I, too, wanted to quit, and move back to Oregon. I felt I could no longer give my full attention to work.

Eric had given me Maxine's phone number so I kept in touch with her regularily. Maxine had given me Twyla's phone number, so I could call her. When I did call Twyla, I asked her if she would be going back to Maxine's in the near future. Twyla said she had to work the weekends and would be unable to go back for another month.

I found myself talking to Maxine, over the phone, on a regular basis. I talked with Twyla on several occasions as well. Twyla invited me to her house in Wileetka, to stay a weekend whenever I wanted. I jumped at the chance thinking the spirit, or whatever it was, might be at her house.

I stayed a weekend in early February 1998, with Twyla, Steve, and the kids however, nothing happened at their house. Since Twyla was central to the haunting at Maxine's, I hoped that there might be some activity at her house. The house was quiet the entire weekend I stayed. Twyla explained that very little happened at her house that had anything to do with spirits.

Just one week after staying at Steve and Twyla's house, I gave Don my two weeks notice. I told Don, and Eric, I wanted to move back to Oregon. I was no longer interested in the type of work I was doing. Eric quit working for Don around the same time. During my last two weeks working for Don, I saw less and less of Eric. I considered him to be one of my best friends; however, we had started to drift apart. I sensed that Eric was upset that I was moving back to Oregon.

Two days before I was to leave for Oregon, I called Twyla and Maxine and told them good-bye. I had thought of staying in Oklahoma, and trying a different type of employment, but I wanted to see my family and friends. Maxine, and Twyla, were both disappointed that I was leaving. I told them not to worry, one day in the not so distant future I would pull up in Maxine's driveway and surprise them with my return.

I left Oklahoma on a cold, snowy night in late February of 1998. The drive back took three days. I had plenty of time, during the drive back to Oregon, to think hard about my experiences over the last fifteen months. I had not talked with my brother, Tracy, in quite some time. I could not bring myself to call and say I was moving back to Oregon. Deep down I realized that I owed him many thanks for his part in my coming to Oklahoma. If not for his invitation to come and stay with him, I would have never met Maxine, Twyla, and Eric, and I would not have experienced the unknown.

While I was thinking about Eric, during the trip back to Oregon, I suddenly realized I had not told him good-bye. In the coming years, that oversight would come back to haunt me.

FIVE

In June 1998, four months after leaving Oklahoma, the experiences I had at Maxine's were still on my mind. The memories of the experiences were so ever present in my subconscious mind that they would easily surface to a vivid conscious level, with the slightest mention of Oklahoma. They would also resurface if I happened to be flipping through channels on the television and came across a show about ghosts.

I was working two jobs. I worked as a supervisor at the Station Restaurant, and as a desk clerk at the Harbor View Motel. Both places are located in the small, cozy village of Bandon Oregon. Bandon is nestled along the Southern Oregon Coast, at the mouth of the Coquille River. At one time, Bandon was a booming fishing port that later became defunct due to two major factors: One factor was that the Army Corps of Engineers built the jetty to protect the fishing vessels from high waves entering the port, but didn't dredge the sediment from the bar, which made the bar too treacherous to cross. The other major headache for the fisherman was that the abundance of fish in the ocean had disappeared. The federal Government had to set guidelines that limited the amount and types of fish that could be caught. The treacherous bar, and the lack of fish left the commercial fishing industry in ruin. Today, the town is a popular tourist attraction. People come from all over to enjoy the pristine beaches, and take advantage of the many shops and restaurants in Bandon's Old Town.

During the summer that year, I was working about seventy hours a week. I didn't have much time for friends or family, but I somehow managed to find the time to meet a wonderful woman who had three children. Linda was tall, thin, and had long beautiful brown hair. From the very moment we met, I could tell by her comforting personality, that she was a loving and caring person, and also a wonderful mother. Linda's children, Devin eight years old, Haley five, and Mara just eighteen months, seemed to take a liking to me. We spent a lot of time enjoying each others company and in December of 1998, we moved into an apartment together.

Linda and I got along pretty well until late February of 1999, when Linda noticed that I was acting strangely. Our apartment was well lived in, but always clean, however on a daily basis I was running frantically throughout the house picking up toys from off the floor, and putting dishes, cups and glasses, in the sink that had been lying around. This type of behavior was not normal for me, and I had no immediate explanation for my obsession. My behavior was so obsessive compulsive that when Linda or one of the kids finished their meals, or drinking water or soda, I would immediately gather up their dishes and wash them. Linda had always kept the house clean, but for some reason it was never clean enough for me.

By May of 1999, my obsessive behavior had gotten worse. Linda and I were arguing every day that month, but we loved each other enough to try and find a solution to my problem. Linda was a very forgiving person and was willing to help me get through this difficult time. Then it hit me, I was thinking about Maxine and that I hadn't spoken with her in quite some time. While I was thinking about her, I remembered what I had witnessed, and the objects that had been hurled at me, while I was at her house. Could the experiences that I had at Maxine's be the cause my obsessive compulsive behavior? Was it possible that the spirit "Michael" was having an adverse affect on me? These were very real possibilities and the only logical explanation I had for my strange behavior. For the first time, I told Linda about what I had witnessed while I was at Maxine's however, she did not believe that a spirit was the cause of my strange behavior.

In early June, while working an evening shift at the motel, I decided to tell my story of the experiences I had at Maxine's to my manager, Jodi Grundy. Jodi and I had become good friends during the time that I had worked at the motel. As I told her about the strange activity that I had witnessed at Maxine's house, her eyes grew wide with amazement. I also mentioned my strange behavior at home. Jodi agreed that my experiences at Maxine's most likely caused my eccentric behavior at home. When I was finished telling her my story, she told me that she had on several occasions, seen ghosts in her house. She said that one night, she was awakened by what she described, as an apparition, standing near her bed.

"The first time that I saw the apparition, I just dismissed it because I thought I was seeing things," Jodi said. "After that experience I would see and hear people walking around upstairs at the motel when I lived there in 1995. I couldn't understand what I was seeing and hearing, because I was the only one upstairs at the time."

I told Jodi that I was not entirely convinced that the haunting at Maxine's was in fact real, yet I had no explanation for the strange events that I had witnessed. Jodi told me she didn't believe in ghosts at first, but after what she had seen and heard, she definitely believed in ghosts now.

During the month of August 1999, Linda, the kids, and I, went camping at Sixes River Oregon, located about seventeen miles south of Bandon. The Sixes River, runs through the coastal mountains of southern Oregon, to it's final destination, the ocean. It is very scenic with lots of wildlife and beautiful tall trees. Wayne, and Samantha Chandler, along with their six children Marissa, Sheena, Falon, Courtney, Jordan, and Hayley, were going camping and having a birthday party. We set up camp early and swam in the river most of the day.

By nightfall, we had a large fire going and hamburgers on the grill. After dinner, our two families huddled around the campfire to continue a long tradition of telling ghost stories. Generations of indigenous elders, trappers, pioneers and scout masters had over the years told their ghost tales around their own campfires. This campfire was no different, with the children begging the adults to tell a ghost story. We went around the campfire listening to each adult tell their scary story. Although the stories being told were make believe, they were exciting to hear. I was the last to tell my tale, and before I started, I warned everyone that this would be no ordinary ghost story. I began by telling everyone how I was first introduced to Maxine and her family. While I was telling them about the strange occurrences that I had personally witnessed at Maxine's house, I noticed the kids huddling closer and closer to each other. Their eyes grew bigger and bigger as piece by piece, the story of the haunting at Maxine's captured the small but attentive audience. At the end of my story, the kids asked if I had seen a ghost, or if I believed that the house was haunted. My response to them was this: I had never seen a ghost in my entire life, nor did I believe that they existed, but I was unable to explain any of the strange things that had happened at Maxine's house. I would let those around the campfire decide whether or not the haunting that I had witnessed, was real.

When we woke the next morning, Samantha, said she was upset with me because of the story I had told the night before. She told me that her children, who did not sleep well, were frightened by my story. I listened to what Samantha was saying to me and I understood her concerns for her children. I apologized to her and explained that I wasn't aware that my story would affect the children in a bad way. After talking with Samantha, I realized that my experiences affected me by altering my behavior, so I should have known that my story could affect the children by scaring them. Later that day, I asked Linda if she had noticed if her children were frightened by my story. Linda told me that the kids slept well the previous night and that they didn't seem to be affected in any way.

Things were going better for Linda and me by September of that year. We were engaged to be married and had set a date of November 22nd, 1999. My behavior had started to improve during that time, and I thought it was because I was able to get my story out in the open. Each time that I would tell of my experiences at Maxine's, I felt a therapeutic healing come over me. Linda also noticed a change for the better, in my behavior.

On my birthday, October 23rd, I called Maxine for the first time since I had left Oklahoma. Maxine told me that Bill was now in a nursing home, and that Twyla and Steve had moved closer to her and were living just eight miles from her in the small rural community of Colgate. I asked her if she had heard from Eric and if he had been to Centrahoma to see her since I had left. "Eric hasn't been here since you two were run out of my house that night before you left to go back to Oregon." I really felt like a family member when Maxine asked me when I could come and see her again. I told her that I was getting married next month and that I would be a stepfather to her three children. Now that I was going to have a family I wasn't sure when I would be able to afford to come back to Oklahoma. Before our conversation ended, I told her to tell Twyla and Steve "Hi" and that I would hopefully see everyone again someday.

In January of 2000, things were beginning to slow down at my two jobs. The tourist season had wound down to practically nothing. I quit working at the restaurant that month, but continued working full-time at the motel. I had not thought about Maxine or Eric, since I had talked to them last. My compulsive behavior was still there, but getting better, which I thought was because I was telling my story and getting it off my chest. That all changed one day in early February, when I received an unlikely phone call from my brother, Guy, who lived in Incline Village, Nevada.

The phone call from Guy was unlikely because he never called his family. Guy was the type of person who enjoyed a private lifestyle. He would call only if he wanted to talk with you. He called me because he wanted to know if I would be interested in starting a business with him. The last time that we spoke, I had mentioned to him that I had gone to Oklahoma and that I had worked as a process server. This time, it was Guy who brought up the subject of Oklahoma, which immediately brought back the memories of Maxine's house. Guy told me that he had some money to invest and wanted to know if I thought Oklahoma would be a good place to start a business. I told him about process serving in Oklahoma, and that if I decided to go back to that type of work, Oklahoma would be an advantageous place to start. I told him that I knew the area well. Guy said that he only wanted to be an investor; he didn't want to work the business. He asked me to consider his proposition, and call him when I made a decision. I told him I would get back to him within a month.

One month after talking with Guy on the phone, my obsessive behavior, which I thought was under control, had returned. Once again, Linda and I struggled to deal with my problem, only this time, it was worse than before. Along with my frantic cleaning frenzy, I would also get verbally hostile with Linda and the kids. I did not know why at the time, but I started telling Linda every day that I needed to get back to Maxine's house. Because I had told Linda what I had gone through at Maxine's, she understood, but she did not want me to leave her and the kids. I felt the same way, but I could no longer suppress the memories of my experiences, nor could I control my need to find a logical explanation for the haunting at Maxine's house.

I feel that each of us is put on this earth for a purpose. Was it my purpose to involve myself in finding the answer, or even just to understand what was happening at Maxine's? The answer was simple; I believed that I had finally found my purpose in life.

I called Guy in late February, and told him that I was interested in starting the business. With a feeling of deception in my heart, I suggested we start the business in Oklahoma. At that time, Linda and Guy had no idea what I was really planning. I knew that by going back to Oklahoma for reasons other than starting a business, I would be deceiving Linda, Guy, and myself. Because my behavior was getting worse, I thought this was my only hope to cure my obsession. I also thought that Linda might need some time away from me because I had not been an easy person to live with.

I waited until September of 2000, to tell Linda of my plans. I waited that long because I was worried about what her reaction might be. I tried to convince Linda that if the business worked out we could make a lot of money. "I don't care about the money, the kids and I would rather have you home," she said. I wanted to tell Linda the real reason I wanted to go back to Oklahoma, but even though she might have understood, I knew that she wouldn't let me go. Linda would not want to be left alone, but did not want to relocate her and the kids in case the business didn't work out. Linda agreed to support my decision on the condition that I would work hard to make my business venture successful, but if the business was not working out after one month, I was to come home. I told Linda that I would do my best to succeed. One thing that I was certain about was if Linda found out that I was deceiving her, she would never trust me again. Because of my behavior, and relentless desire to get back to Oklahoma, I was starting to believe that "Michael", did indeed exist. I actually felt like Michael's spirit was inside me, guiding me back to Oklahoma.

For the next two months I researched a good location in Oklahoma for our business. I called several County courthouses in different areas of Oklahoma, to find out how many process servers were licensed in each area. I found that Stillwater, at the time, had the fewest licensed servers; there were only five. Stillwater had a population of around thirty five thousand people, which included the students who lived on campus at Oklahoma State University. There were also several other large towns close by, which provided a large population base, making this an ideal business opportunity.

The Christmas holiday was just two weeks away and Linda and I were busy shopping for the kids. We spent quality family time together, even more so than in the past, knowing that I was planning to leave for Oklahoma in three weeks. Linda and the kids were excited about Christmas, but sad that I was leaving.

On the night of January 1st 2001, I said good-bye to Linda and the kids, got in the car, and drove away. While driving to Oklahoma, I didn't think about the business at all, but only about my plans to unravel the mystery that plagued not only the Mcwethy family, but my family too.

During the drive, my conscience was bothering me. I felt like I was a compulsive gambler using someone else's money. I was going to start a business, knowing full well, the money could be lost without making a profit. At that moment, I decided that I would try to give one hundred percent to both ventures. If I failed at either endeavor, I would at the least have the peace of mind of knowing that I tried.

I reached Stillwater, Oklahoma in the early morning hours of January 4th. I got a motel and slept the rest of that day. I spent the next seven days locating an apartment, getting business cards made up, and applying for my license to serve legal papers. While waiting for my license to be approved I solicited several attorneys' offices most of which told me that they already had a process server, which made me realize that I had my work cut out for me. I had previously researched the area and had not planned for any such setbacks. My license was granted on Thursday January 11th. That same day I had also found an apartment in which I would not only live, but use for an office as well.

Since attorneys' wheels of justice don't turn on weekends, I decided to pay a visit to the Mcwethy family on Friday evening, January 12th.

The time was seven thirty, when I blessed the family with my presence. No pun intended, but by the look on Maxine's face when she opened the front door, you would have thought she was looking at a ghost.

"Jason, why didn't you call and tell us you were coming?" she asked, giving me a big hug.

"I wanted to surprise you Maxine." I couldn't believe my eyes when I entered the house. Eric, Twyla, Steve and the kids were all there. It was like a family reunion. I wasn't too surprised to see Twyla and her family, but Eric on the other hand, hadn't been a regular visitor since I had left in 1998. Maxine was in total awe finding it hard to believe that Eric and I would show up at her house on the same day.

"What are you doing here Eric?" I had to ask knowing the odds of Eric and I being here on the same day was a million to one. Eric had no idea that I was coming. Maxine didn't know that Eric was either. While I was talking to Eric, he seemed aloof, and distant. It was apparent to me that my not saying good-bye, when I left in 1998, was not just water under the bridge. I thought we would be able to pick-up where we left off, I was wrong.

"I hadn't been here for quite some time, and since I was recovering from a surgery that I had a month ago, I wasn't working so I decided to drop in. I have been getting tired more frequently which makes it difficult to drive even short distances."

"What kind of surgery did you have?"

"It's kind of personal, and I don't want to go into any details."

"I understand, and I'm really glad to see you Eric. I hope you get to feeling better."

While we were getting reacquainted, I explained to everyone why I was back in Oklahoma. I told them a little about the business I was starting, but I was much more interested in the ongoing haunting at Maxine's. I wanted Maxine, Twyla, and Eric to know what I wanted to accomplish while I was here; I would try to find an explanation for the haunting. If Michael was a true spirit, I would also try to find out why he choose Twyla to be the central figure that allowed him to manifest himself through her. I wanted to take a closer look at all of the newspaper articles, pictures, or anything else involving the haunting that Maxine had around her house. I wanted to see if I had overlooked anything that might explain some of the strange events that had occurred over the years.

Eric would only stay an hour that night, after I arrived. He said that he needed to go home, because he was starting to get tired. Before Eric left I apologized for not saying good-bye to him when I left Oklahoma in 1998. I felt I owed him that because Eric and I had been good friends. Eric didn't show as much excitement about investigating the haunting as he had in the past. He was definitely adamant about not staying the night. By the way Eric was looking over his shoulders, and the way his eyes were wandering around the room, it was clear to me that he was still very much affected by being run out of Maxine's house. Before Eric left, I told him good-bye and that I hoped to see him again.

I stayed that night at Maxine's and experienced much of the same kinds of activities that I had witnessed in the past. While Steve was sleeping, he was hit with a bottle of lotion that seemed to explode all over the blankets he slept under. He also had a tube of toothpaste that was squeezed into his hair. Moments after that, two eggs were hurled through the darkened living room, followed by a squirt of syrup that created a wavy like design on one of the walls. This was nothing new. Steve received the worst end of the onslaught that night. Steve reacted like he always did, cursing Michael, and asking, "Why me?

The following morning, after reading some of the articles about the haunting, I began to discover what I thought was a pattern to some of this madness: First of all, most of the items that had been hurled at individuals over the years, were directed only at the adult males who were present. Second, and probably more significant than anything, almost all of the activity occurred when one or more of the males was in the company of Twyla. I had that pattern in mind, when I asked Maxine if I could stay at her house on the weekends to try to analyze the haunting more closely. "You can stay anytime you like Jason," she said.

During the time that I spent away from Maxine's, I worked diligently on my business. Although I wasn't making much money, I felt there was still a chance that the business would succeed. Money was tight and I only had enough from Guy's investment to sustain myself for a month. Guy and I had agreed that if the money ran out, and the business was not profiting, there would be no further investment from him

I called Linda often while I was in Oklahoma, and told her that the business was not doing well. Linda was supportive, knowing that I was doing the best that I could. Every time we spoke, and I would ask how her and the kids were doing, and Linda would say that everyone was okay. "Just concentrate on you're business," she would tell me. We didn't talk much about Maxine's house because I didn't want her to think I wasn't working hard to make the business successful.

On Friday, January 19th, I went back to Maxine's to stay the weekend. That particular weekend Maxine and I were the only two at her house. Twyla and Steve had to work so they couldn't stay with us. I was hoping that Eric would call Maxine and come over to stay the night, but we never heard from him. "Eric must not feel too well Jason, or he would be here," Maxine told me.

"Maxine, I asked Eric about his surgery and he didn't want to elaborate about it; I think he is still mad at me."

After tossing and turning in bed for an hour that night, I started hearing voices, which I thought were coming from the front yard. I could not understand what they were saying. It sounded like two, maybe three people talking in loud voices. I looked out the window and did not see anyone. The voices seemed to originate from the front yard. I put on my jacket and walked outside to see if anyone was in the yard, but by this time, the voices had stopped. I walked completely around the house, checked the garage and extra room behind the house, and could find nobody outside. I went back into the house thinking that maybe there were some people walking down the street talking, but again, I saw no one. No sooner did I get back to sleep, the voices started again. This time I heard a large group of people talking and laughing. I looked out the front window and could see nothing.

The next morning I asked Maxine if she had heard any voices the night before. "I did not hear anything," she replied. I explained to Maxine what I had heard the previous night. Maxine told me that the voices might have come from the house across the street, because they are often outside talking. "I went outside and didn't see anyone at all, Maxine." By the strange look that I got from Maxine, I could tell she had no answer that would satisfy my curiosity about the voices that I had heard.

During that day, I looked at several photographs that were taken by Maxine over the years concerning the haunting. One picture in particular caught my eye. The picture showed a message drawn out on the floor, in bird gravel. The message was a series of squiggly lines that began with the letter "M" followed by a connecting line of twists and turns that appeared to cover about three square feet. I thought that there was some significance concerning the letter "M" in the drawing. Maybe Michael was trying to tell the family that it was he, who made the drawing.

"Maxine, has anyone tried to decipher this message written in bird gravel?"

"A fellow by the name of Mark Russell came to our house to interview my family and also looked at the picture; he felt that the spirit was sending a message, but he didn't know what the message meant. After he interviewed both Twyla, and me concerning all of the activity that went on around the house, he wrote a book called *"Testament."* The book was mainly written from several interviews that Mr. Russell conducted with my family. The book also covered religious topics."

The other pictures that I looked at were what some would call cryptograms. A cryptogram is a message or writing in code or cipher. It is also an occult symbol or representation. The first picture of a cryptogram, taken at Maxine's house on February 7th, 1993, was a drawing that looked like an anchor. It was found on a mirror in the house. The next cryptogram appeared just six days later, on February 13th, 1993. This one was drawn in red lipstick on a mirror in one of Maxine's bedrooms. The cryptogram looked like a child's rendition of a stickman with the arms raised over the head. The drawing also included an arrow that pointed away from the drawing.

I studied these cryptograms at great length, but I could not figure out what they meant. I concluded that any child could have drawn these pictures. This led me to believe that if Michael had created these drawings, then what Maxine has said all along, that Michael is a small child, must be true.

I left Maxine's house on Sunday, January 21st, with what I thought was a small piece of the puzzle in place. I really felt like I was making some progress. I couldn't help but wonder why I seemed to be the only one who wanted to solve this mystery of the haunting. Since the first night I was introduced to Maxine and her family, I noticed that everyone who lived at the house, and those who visited her house, never took an interest in figuring out why these strange things were happening. Personally, I was very glad to have the opportunity to be involved with this haunting, and maybe get the chance to understand this phenomena. I think the reason Maxine and her family, and the people who witnessed the haunting, didn't want to find an explanation, was because they may have thought the haunting would stop.

Three weeks passed, and in that time, I had only served about thirty papers. I was getting twenty dollars per paper, which totaled around six hundred dollars. I was not making enough money to support two households, and I was really stressed.

On Thursday, February 11th, I received a phone call from Richard Harris, my former employer in Oregon. The conversation was short and to the point: "Jason, would you like to come back to work at the Harbor View Motel?" Before I could answer, I was told that the new job would be in management, and would include a raise in pay, and a bonus. I would be supervising housekeeping, and maintenance. I told Richard that I needed a few days to think it over and would call him with my decision. After speaking with Richard, I called Linda to see how she felt, Linda said in a positive tone, "It's you're decision to make and I'll support you with whatever you decide."

Since I had no papers to serve for the next few days, I went to Maxine's Friday night, February 12th. When I arrived at her house, she, Twyla, and her children were just finishing dinner. I told Maxine that I might be going back to Oregon, because I wasn't making enough money in Oklahoma. I told her about a phone call I received concerning a job offer. Maxine really wanted me to stay in Oklahoma, but she also understood that I needed to be able to support my family. "We have become like family Jason; I hate to see you leave," Twyla said, her voice cracking.

The house that night was unusually quiet. With Twyla present, I expected strange things would happen. At about one o'clock in the morning I was awakened by a loud SLAP! Followed by a scream, and then crying. I immediately looked toward the direction of the slap and saw Twyla and Meagan, who was seven years old at the time, sitting upright on the hide-a-bed. I got up from the couch to find out what was happening. When I turned the light on, I saw that Meagan's right cheek was red and swollen. Twyla was asking Meagan, "Are you okay, who did this to you, who slapped you in the face?" Meagan kept saying she didn't know what happened. "I have something in my eye," she said to Twyla. When Meagan took her hand from over her eye, Twyla saw that her right eye was covered with Vaseline. Twyla cleaned the Vaseline out of Meagan's eye and kept repeating over and over, "I can't believe Michael would do this to Meagan."

I asked Twyla if she heard the slap, which she said, "Yes, Meagan and I were whispering about something, which I can't remember now, and when I turned over facing away from her, I heard a slap." Twyla seemed more angry than upset. I was wondering why Kelsey, who was sleeping with Maxine, did not wake up from all of the commotion when just then, Maxine walked into the living room. Twyla told Maxine what had happened. With a inquiring look, Maxine commented, "Michael has never done anything like this to the kids. Why would he do it now?" I was wondering the same thing.

The next morning Twyla, Meagan, Kelsey, and I left Maxine's to pick some things up from Twyla's house. On the way to Twyla's house I was struck in the back of my head with a small, hard plastic dollhouse. The dollhouse must have come from the back seat area where the kids were sitting, but I knew they wouldn't throw anything in the car because if they did, Twyla would reprimand them. It didn't really hurt, but it definitely startled me. "Michael is at it again Twyla," I said, shaking my head.

Just before we got to Twyla's house a thought suddenly popped into my head: Right before I was struck with the doll house, Twyla and I were talking about me going back to Oregon. I started to think about all of the times I was at Maxine's when strange things would occur: Who was present, and what the topic of conversation was at the time? I was struck by the realization that whenever someone was hit with an object, Twyla was present, and the people present were conversing about a subject other than the haunting or spirit. But, if they were talking about Michael, nothing would happen. These thoughts raised several questions: Is this spirit jealous because he is not getting our full attention? Does the spirit only wish to have Twyla all to himself? Why, in most cases, does the spirit attack only male adults? Other than Meagan, who was assaulted the night before, males who are in the company of Twyla, especially when they are at Maxine's house, seem to be the main target for the spirit's aggressions. These questions, I felt, were pointing to the answers I was seeking.

After we arrived at Twyla's house, I asked if I could use the restroom. Twyla directed me down the hall to the first door on the left. As I was about to enter the bathroom, I noticed four lines of a dark red liquid, that were about three inches in length, dripping down the middle of the door. It looked like blood dripping from the door, and it looked fresh. Nobody had been at Twyla's house since the day before. I called for Twyla, to come and look. Twyla looked at the red liquid running down the door, and didn't seem surprised it was there. I thought her reaction was due to the fact that so many strange things had happened over the years that this was no different. I bent down to get a closer look, and then ran my finger through the liquid and put it to my nose, I could smell a strong scent of iron. "Twyla, this is blood," I told her. She reacted simply by getting a towel and wiping it off the door. We left her house shortly after that and went back to Maxine's. On the way to Maxine's, I kept asking myself the same question over and over: Why wasn't Twyla bothered by the blood on her door?

When we arrived at Maxine's I asked Twyla why she didn't seem worried that there was blood dripping from a door in her house. "Jason, that may have been blood on the door, but nothing surprises me anymore because so much has happened since all of this started."

No matter how Twyla felt, I thought that there was definitely a reason for that blood on the door at that precise time. When I told Maxine about what we had found at Twyla's, she wasn't real surprised, either.

When I got back to my apartment in Stillwater, that Sunday night, I couldn't sleep thinking about the discovery I made at Twyla's house. If that really was blood that was on the door at Twyla's house, why did the blood not appear at Maxine's house? I was convinced that Michael was trying to communicate something to me or to Twyla. I couldn't figure out what the four bloody lines on the door meant. Of all the things I had seen Michael do, if in fact it was Michael, this disturbed me the most.

On Monday, February 15th, admitting to myself that my business was not working out as planned, I called Linda and told her that I was going to accept the job at the motel and come home. Linda and the kids were delighted. After talking to Richard Harris, and accepting the job, I called Guy and told him that the business was not making enough money and I was returning to Oregon the following week. I told Guy that I could no longer sustain my expenses in Oklahoma. By the tone in his voice, he was not happy. I could tell he thought that I wasted his money and time, going to Oklahoma. I really could not blame him for being disappointed.

I spent the next week closing out my business and thanking each of my clients for the business I had received from them. They were understanding of my situation and appreciated my efforts.

I called Maxine and told her good-bye, and that I was going back to Oregon. Twyla happened to be at Maxine's when I called, so I spoke with her long enough to tell her good-bye, as well. "I'm sorry that you're business didn't work out for you," she said. "That's okay Maxine," I told her, "I feel like we have made some progress concerning you're situation." Towards the end of our conversation that day I assured Maxine that I would come back to Oklahoma, because I wanted, with her blessing, to further investigate the things that were happening at her house. Maxine was thrilled that I was interested in finding an explanation for the unusual activity that had plagued her family for years. She felt that I was the most determined, because of the interest that I showed, to seek some answers for the haunting.

SIX

Halloween night, Friday, October 31st, 2003, I was working the front desk at the Harbor View Motel in Bandon, Oregon. I was counting down the hours, until my flight left for Oklahoma the next morning. Maxine and I had spoken by phone just two days earlier, and she knew that I was coming for a visit. Twenty months had passed, since my last encounter with Michael. I was anxious, yet cautious, about spending the next four nights at Maxine's house. I was anxious because I wanted to see Maxine and her family, and cautious because I didn't know what to expect concerning how intense Michael's activity would be when I arrived. In the past, the activity became more violent, and more frequent, with each visit. For the last twenty months, I had kept in constant contact with Maxine and her family. I often asked Maxine if the activity from Michael had in any way intensified since my last visit. Maxine told me that Michael is always present, but not always active. "When you least expect it, Michael strike's, without warning."

I got home from work at eleven-fifteen that Friday night. I was in bed at midnight, and tossed and turned until I got up at four-thirty, Saturday morning, to get ready to fly to Oklahoma. I kissed Linda goodbye and drove to the airport. According to my itinerary, I would not land in Oklahoma City until around ten o'clock, that evening.

I soon settled in for the long flight and dozed off so I would be well rested when I got to Maxine's.

My emotions were heightened when I stepped off the plane and entered the Will Rogers airport in Oklahoma City. A reception party of one, Twyla, greeted me at the gate. Twyla's face lit up when she saw me. We said our helloes and left the airport for the two-hour drive to Centrahoma.

We had only been driving for about fifteen minutes when two objects hit the windshield, from inside the car, with tremendous force. I expected to find the windshield cracked from the force of the objects thrown. We found two quarters on the dash of the car immediately after we heard the objects hit the windshield. Just before the quarters hit, we were talking about a friend of Twyla's, Calle. Then Michael made his presence known! Twyla commented that Michael's activity had started sooner than she had anticipated. I thought, oh great, no sleep for me tonight.

At around twelve-thirty, Sunday morning, we pulled into Maxine's driveway. We got out of the car and were greeted by Maxine and four visitors. The four visitors were a middle-aged woman, her daughter who appeared to be in her mid-twenties, and two teenage girls. Maxine, who did not know the people, told them when they arrived to stay until I got to the house. She explained to them that whenever I come to the house, Michael's presence is strong. I was not formally introduced to the visitors, but I was told that they were from the small town of Stonewall, just ten minutes from Centrahoma. The daughter of the middle-aged woman was carrying a video camcorder, and was walking around in the dark collecting video footage of Maxine's property. I could tell by her intense look that she was hoping to record images of a ghost; I did not have the heart to tell her that her camcorder would be useless at this house. I remembered how disappointed I was when my video equipment would not function here.

After a few minutes of standing outside talking in the cool crisp fall weather, everyone, including the new visitors, gathered in Maxine's living room. Present that night were Maxine, Twyla and her three children, the four visitors and myself. Maxine shared her experiences of the haunting with the new visitors, and kept the small audience captivated. I, too, shared my experiences with Michael the spirit, which intensified their interest. I could tell that they were nervous about being in the house, because when I told them about what I had experienced, they clutched each other tightly as if they were on a scary ride at an amusement park. The visitors explained that they were uneasy being in the house.

At around two o'clock, Sunday morning, while everyone was sitting in the living room, several objects hit the walls. The objects turned out to be two quarters, and a penny. The visitors were startled, and became increasingly uncomfortable. The woman said that she was worried someone would get hurt if hit by a large object. The woman, her daughter and the teens, left a few minutes later. Due to the lateness of the hour, Twyla and her kids left shortly after that.

I still felt tired when I awoke at nine-thirty, Sunday morning. I had not slept well because I was excited to be back at Maxine's. I slept with one eye open most of the night, for no other reason than to dodge any incoming objects, if thrown in my direction.

The weather was warm and sunny that day, so at one o'clock I decided to go hiking behind Maxine's property. On top of a hill behind her house is an old oil tank tower that overlooks Centrahoma. I climbed the ladder of the tank tower to the top, which is about twenty feet from the ground, and took several pictures of the town. I had never taken pictures of Centrahoma, and I wanted to show my friends and family back home the town where the restless spirit Michael calls home.

Later that day, I went into the town of Colgate to do some food shopping for Maxine. I wanted to buy groceries for her because she was always very hospitable to me. I felt privileged to be a part of her life and to experience the spirit with whom she shares her home. With the thousands of visitors that make the pilgrimage to Maxine's each year, one has to wonder how many times she has told her story. Maxine always welcomes the visitors with a smile no matter what time of day, or night, they arrive.

After getting back to the house, I put the groceries away and spent the rest of the day talking with Maxine. I told Maxine that I had only a few days to gather as much information as I could, concerning the town and her property. I was adamant about finding a connection, or link to the haunting. I asked her if there was anything that she had not told me in the past that would help me to connect the dots and piece together a plausible theory. At that particular time, Maxine said she couldn't think of anything that she hadn't told me. I would later discover that she had not told me some very crucial details about Michael.

At six o'clock that evening, Twyla returned to Maxine's with her youngest daughter Sidney and asked Maxine if she, Sidney, could stay overnight. Twyla had to go to Ada on Monday morning, and could not take Sidney with her.

"Sure," Maxine said. Maxine loved her grandchildren and she had no problem with Sidney staying the night. Twyla visited with Maxine and me for about an hour, and then left for her home.

Just before I went to bed that night, I placed a small pocket recorder that I had brought with me, on top of the television set. Out of shear curiosity, I wanted to hear what, if anything went on in the house while we slept.

At six-thirty Monday morning, I was awakened by Sidney, who was carrying on a conversation with herself or so I thought. I did not hear Maxine talking to her at the time. I continued to lay in bed and listen to this eight-month old child try to talk, but no one was talking back to her. Sidney was not old enough to put words together that you could understand. Fifteen minutes later, I went into the kitchen and found Maxine sitting at the table reading a newspaper. Sidney was on the kitchen floor next to Maxine.

"Who was Sidney talking to Maxine," I asked jokingly.

"Oh she just rattles to herself," Maxine replied. "I've been reading the paper and listening to her mumble."

"Is that chicken I smell cooking on the stove?" I asked.

"That's what we're having for dinner," Maxine said.

An hour had passed, when I checked the recorder to find out if any unusual noises were recorded over night. I rewound the tape and pushed play... Maxine and I just looked at each other and could not understand what we were hearing. The first five minutes of the tape sounded familiar, like a Star Wars movie, with the main character on this tape being R2D2. We heard a series of "Bleeps, and Boops, along with short, loud, whistles. Everyone who has seen the movie knows the sounds R2D2 makes. We had never heard noises like this in Maxine's house before. Unless Hollywood slipped sound effects into Maxine's house while we slept, we had some visitors! On the last six or seven minutes of the recording, we could hear three adult male voices talking. Each male voice had a different pitch. One voice had a high tone, while the other two sounded deep. The voices faded in and out and were extremely hard to understand. It was almost like listening to three drunks. I managed to catch bits and pieces of the conversation:

"It's okay honey, Yeah, I know, don't worry." During the conversation, the men would often laugh, and towards the end of the recording, I heard Twyla's name mentioned, with a deep whisper, by one of the male voices.

Twyla and her daughter Kelsey, who was three years old, got to Maxine's house at ten o'clock that morning. We asked Twyla to listen to the tape. Twyla's reaction to the recording was slightly different than ours had been. By nature, Twyla never used foul language, but after listening to the tape, all of that went out the window.

"Oh shit! What are those weird noises?" She said looking concerned. "Who the hell is talking on the tape?" She repeated over and over. I thought to myself, maybe there could be more spirits in Maxine's house then just Michael and Leader. We all wondered that same thing. I must have spent at least thirty minutes, telling Maxine and Twyla, how important this recording could be if given to the right people for their opinion. The people I had in mind were those who study this type of preternatural phenomenon. Unfortunately, no one else would ever hear the tape.

It was almost eleven o'clock that morning, when I was sitting at the table and mentioned to Maxine, "I think I'm going to make some sandwiches." I opened the refrigerator, took out some mayonnaise and bologna, laid out four slices of bread, and all hell broke loose! Just when I was about to spread the mayonnaise on the bread, an egg flew right past my head and splattered on the wall in front of me. Maxine and Twyla started laughing at me. Kelsey and Sidney, who were also in the kitchen, were laughing, too. I went to the opposite end of the kitchen to get some paper towels to clean the wall. I grabbed the towels, turned around, and was struck with an uneaten bowl of milk and cereal. Someone must have been eating the cereal before I got out of bed. The bowl of cereal had first hit the ceiling, and then it struck me in the chest, leaving me splattered with milk and cereal. I remembered seeing that bowl of cereal on the table when I first got up that morning. When I looked up, I could see milk dripping from the ceiling. While I was kneeling on the floor, cleaning up the milk, two rolls of pennies struck the back of my head. Twyla, Maxine, Kelsey, and Sidney were now watching from outside the kitchen, in the living room, staying clear of the war zone. I cleaned the egg off the wall, and the milk and cereal from the floor, and I had just started picking up the pennies that were spread all over the kitchen, when I was hit with two plastic glasses full of water. As quickly as it had begun, the assault was over but Michael wasn't quite finished with me just yet.

During the attack, I had called out to Twyla to grab my camera, and take some pictures of what was occurring.

Suddenly, for some reason, I thought about what we had recorded last night. I went to the kitchen table, picked up the recorder, and pushed the eject button, the tape was gone!

"My tape is gone?" I said, looking at Maxine.

"The tape is missing?" she asked, looking surprised. "Oh, I'll bet that Michael got your tape," she said.

Moments later, while Maxine was standing over the stove, she started to snicker, "I found your tape Jason," Maxine shouted.

"Where?" I asked her.

"It's in this pot of chicken." I quickly stepped over to the stove and looked inside the pot. There, floating in what was supposed to be dinner, I found what was left of the tape. One could easily imagine how upset I was when I pulled the tape from the boiling pot of chicken, and found that the recording was destroyed; the tape had melted.

"All I can say is someone besides us knew how important this tape was." I told Maxine and Twyla.

I sat down at the kitchen table and put my head in my hands. I muttered to myself, "I could sure use a cigarette right now." Just as I looked up, I saw my pack of cigarettes there on the table. The cigarettes had been cut in half! I picked up the cigarette pack and could clearly see that it had been cut with a serrated knife. What really baffled me was that seconds later, I found a steak knife on top of Maxine's four- foot high freezer, next to the refrigerator. There were bits of tobacco on the knife blade and on the freezer. It appeared that my cigarettes were moved from the kitchen table, cut in half on the freezer, and then placed back on the kitchen table, ten feet away. I know that I had put the cigarettes on the kitchen table the night before.

Other mischievous activity began to surface: First, when Maxine opened her fish tank to feed her fish, she found an egg sitting on the bottom of the tank. Second, on Maxine's stove sat three empty spice jars with different colored lids. Until that moment, there had been nothing peculiar about them. Upon looking at the jars more closely, we noticed that inside each jar was a two inch-piece of celery stalk. These celery stalks had been positioned so that if you looked at the jars from the front view, you could clearly see the letter "M." These small, but mischievous acts clearly suggested to me that Michael was not only intelligent, but witty, too!

At one thirty that afternoon, I drove to Colgate. When I got to town, I stopped at the museum and spoke with a pleasant, elderly woman. I asked her if she had any historical documentation concerning possible spirits, or haunting relating to the town of Centrahoma. After searching for a few minutes, the woman handed me a small book entitled, *Ghost Towns of Oklahoma*. This book, which was compiled by the Coal County museum, had stories on several small towns throughout Oklahoma. I looked in the index and found Centrahoma. The book had just eight pages of information on Centrahoma, dating back to the town's original inception. Before the town was called Centrahoma, it had been known by two other names, and occupied three other locations: The first name given to the ghost town on March 3rd, 1892 was Byrd, named after the governor of the Choctaw Indian Nation. Byrd was located just one mile southeast of the present townsite of Tupelo, which is four miles northwest of the present location of Centrahoma. On July 10th 1894, the town Byrd was moved to a new location, and the name was changed to Owl, and that location is unknown. Owl was moved to Centrahoma's present location in 1904, and on July 11th 1907, the town Owl was changed to Centrahoma. There was no information about why the town had relocated several times. The school that the children attended was located in Centrahoma. Many of the school records from that time do not exist, and no records for the town itself could be found for the years, 1905-1908. I read through the information that was available but found nothing I could use. I could not find one person in the town's history with the first name Michael, which, being such a common name seemed strange to me. At one time, Centrahoma had sixteen businesses, and a population of around four hundred. At present, no businesses exist, and the town has fewer than one hundred people.

My next stop was the abstract office that dealt with the land in the area. I wanted to find information about the previous owners of Maxine's property. I was told by a woman at the abstract office, the information I requested would take several weeks to locate, and would cost me several hundred dollars to obtain, which I could not afford. I would have to get the information I needed some other way. It was getting late, so I decided that I would check the newspaper, the Colgate Record, the next day, for any articles about Centrahoma's early day's, that may tie into my investigation.

I got back to Maxine's late that afternoon, and fixed a plate of the chicken dumplings she had made: The same chicken dinner in which my tape had been cooked. I figured that the dinner would be okay because it was fully cooked. I poured a cup of left over coffee and put it in the microwave to heat. When I took the hot coffee out of the microwave, I noticed a bluish powder floating in the cup, upon closer inspection, I found that someone had put Ajax in my coffee. Maxine ate around the same time I did. By six o'clock that evening, we were both feeling sick. Our symptoms were similar: Nausea, vomiting, muscle aches and fever. This type of illness was unusual for me; I rarely get sick. I rested for the remainder of the day. Maxine was ill the entire night. The next day, I was still sick and could not go to the newspaper as planned. Unbeknownst to Maxine and me Michael had one more prank to play.

Everyone who is familiar with my daily routine knows that I drink coffee, lots of coffee. Maxine also enjoys drinking coffee, so what better prank to play on someone than to take something away that they like? At around seven o'clock that evening, Maxine asked if I knew where the can of coffee was. I told her that I had no idea, and had not seen the coffee since that morning. We searched everywhere in the kitchen, and throughout the house. We could not find the coffee. I got in the car and went to the store to buy more. When I returned, I saw the can of coffee sitting on Maxine's roof! A fitting end to my visit, I concluded, and for Michael, he had gotten one last laugh our my expense.

The next morning, Wednesday, I said goodbye to Maxine. Twyla took me to the airport where I told her goodbye and boarded the plane. On the flight back to Oregon, I felt that this visit was too short. I did not feel confident that I was any closer to solving the mystery. This puzzle had something missing, something that I was overlooking. I reminded myself that I was just an amateur in the world of ghost hunting. I did not know it then, but just two weeks later, the final pieces to this intriguing story would come together.

When my plane landed in Oregon, I was weak from the chicken and audio-tape dumplings, and I still had some nausea. I could not help but wonder if Michael had put something more than just a cassette-tape in that pot of chicken.

Saturday evening, November 15th, at seven o'clock, I was working at the motel when I got a call from Eric Smith. He had called me from outside Maxine's house. His breathing sounded erratic over the phone. He told me that he was at Maxine's, and rocks were hitting the walls around him. Twyla and Maxine were also in the house during the attack. Eric said that he tried to leave the house and get in his truck, but the assault followed him outside. Small and medium size rocks were pelting his truck and hitting him as he tried to open his truck door. While he was still talking to me on the phone, he ran back into the house to take cover from the attack. I could hear Twyla screaming. Then Eric handed the phone to Maxine. During my short conversation with Maxine, I could hear objects bouncing off the walls.

"Michael's going crazy," she said. I could also hear Twyla crying and saying in a loud voice, "I don't want to leave mom here alone tonight." Eric got back on the phone and I told him that everyone should get in their cars and leave the house, "good idea," he said, and hung up the phone.

Less than an hour later, the phone rang at the motel again. It was Eric. "Jason," he said, "the rocks have stopped hitting the walls, but the lights in the house are going out one by one." I asked Eric why they were still at the house. He told me that after we spoke everything had returned to normal, and everyone decided to stay, but that was until the lights started flickering throughout the house. He told me that he was worried because the house now had only one working light. I suggested to Eric that everyone should stay at Twyla's house until morning. He said that he would call back in a few hours, and let me know what they decided.

Eric never called me back, but the next day Sunday, a message was left on my answering machine. Along with that message, plus new revelations from Maxine later that day, the investigation would take a new turn.

On Sunday morning, around ten-thirty, Linda asked me if someone had called, because there was a message on the answering machine. We did not hear the phone ring, but according to the date and time on the answering machine, we must have received a call that morning. I was sitting on the edge of our bed when Linda played the message. The message lasted only about fifteen seconds, but what it contained was disturbing to hear. The message was in two parts: The first part was the sound of someone gasping for air, and then being pushed under water while the voice of a man, was shouting in an angry tone. I heard the first voice say "NO!" The first part then faded out and the second part came in. The second part of the message sounded like a person splashing in water while continuing to gasp for air. The voice of the man shouting seemed to be a background voice, while the person gasping for air, who I could not identify as male or female, was more in the foreground, and distinct. After listening to the message about twenty times, I was convinced that Linda and I had been listening to a drowning, and possibly something even more sinister, a murder. I am no expert in technical sound equipment, but I was convinced this message was genuine. Right away I wondered: Who could have sent this message, and why?

I called Maxine an hour later, and told her about the message I had received. I had a strange feeling that there was a connection between the message and Maxine's house. We had never before received a phone message like this one. The call to Maxine opened the gate to some startling new revelations.

I began by trying to describe the message I had received, but that was hard to do, so I let her listen to it instead. After she heard the message she said nervously, "Oh Lord Jason, I've got some things to tell you." She said that Michael had told her and Twyla several years ago, that he was killed by his parents, and then buried in her backyard under the clothesline.

"Why didn't you tell me this before," I asked.

"Jason, Michael has told me so many things over the years that sometimes the things he says, are difficult to believe."

I asked Maxine, if there could be some connection with respect to water, because this sounded like a drowning.

"I have a well in my backyard near the cellar; I keep the well covered so the kids won't fall in."

I then asked the obvious question: Has Michael ever said how, or when, he died?

"He told us he died in 1951."

I told Maxine that if it was Michael who left the message, he might be trying to communicate to me, the circumstances of his death. "Maxine, should we dig under your clothesline?" I asked her.

The phone went silent for a moment, "Jason, if Michael is buried in my backyard, and we find him, I'm afraid he won't visit us anymore."

I told Maxine that maybe Michael wants some closure, so that he can finally rest. "Let's just think about this Maxine, and I will call you later."

"Oh Maxine, just one more question, who lived in the house before you did?"

"The wilkison's did" she replied. Maxine continued, "The house and property has been in the Flatt family since as far back as the 1940's, the wilkison's are related to the Flatts. I asked the granddaughter of Mr. Flatt, sherry, who currently lives next door to me, if anything strange as far as ghosts or haunting, had ever occurred there, and she said no. Sherry does not like to talk about what goes on at my house."

"Is the grandfather, Mr. Flatt still living?" I asked.

"No" Maxine answered, "He died some years back."

"Would Sherry mind if I asked her some questions regarding your house and when she lived there?"

"Jason" she said, the Wilkison's seem to think that I brought Michael with me when I moved into this house. They especially don't like all the people visiting my house day and night. They do not want anything to do with spirits or haunting. I do not think they will speak with you concerning this matter."

"Thanks for the information Maxine," I told her, "if you think of anything else, let me know and I will call you later." I never tried to interview the Wilkison's, respecting their privacy.

I was emotional after listening to the message and talking with Maxine. I have heard of psychics who claim to have received messages from the dead, but I am not a psychic. I had to question my role in this mysterious haunting, which for Maxine and her family has already lasted fourteen years. I also had to ask myself, if the message came from Michael, what course of action should I take now. I was sure of one thing: I believed Michael sent me that message, and that he trusted me enough to confide in me. While thinking about what I had experienced concerning the haunting, and what I know of Maxine and her family, a theory began to take shape.

A few days later, I called the Colgate Record to see if in fact, an article was written concerning the death of a small child in 1951. I was told by the Editorial Department, that no records could be found to substantiate what Maxine told me about Michael's death. I was not too surprised to hear that.

After several weeks of trying to record the message that I had received at home, from the answering machine to a separate recorder, like any of the other evidence I collected, that too, was gone. We had a severe thunderstorm hit the coast and a power failure erased the message.

THE THEORY

Why did Michel attach himself to the Mcwethy family, moreover Twyla, and not some other family in Centrahoma? How has Michael's spirit managed to stay around for all of these years? Who, or what caused Michael's death, and how? Who is Leader, and was he ever present when the strange activity occurred?

The answer to these questions is based purely upon speculation, and like anything else, can be subjected to many different interpretations:

I believe that Twyla herself, although she was not aware at the time, was somewhat responsible for Michael's manifestation. Twyla, at the time of Michael's arrival, was a loving mother to her then only child, Desiree, which attracted Michael to her. When Michael first made is presence known, Twyla was just seventeen years of age. After speaking with Twyla at great length, and researching what I found concerning Poltergeists and how they manifest themselves through an "Agent," with the "Agent" possibly suffering repressed anger or hostility, I could not find that she had any repressed anger or hostility when the haunting began. This led me to concur that a Poltergeist was not the cause of the strange activity at the Mcwethy home. Twyla was a normal teenager with all the same problems that teens have at that age. One significant difference in Twyla's case however, stands out; She had a daughter, two years of age, at the time the haunting started. The fact that she was a mother further supports my belief that Michael is a spirit of the dead who longed for her affection. I also believe that Michael's parents were not as loving and caring as Twyla or the Mcwethys; the Mcwethy family provided the perfect atmosphere in which Michael could exist in a spiritual form.

One aspect of this case has fascinated me almost from the beginning: During my many absences from the Mcwethy house, there were long periods of time that passed, where no activity from the spirit Michael occurred. Suddenly, I would call Maxine and Twyla, and tell them I would be coming for a visit soon, and that one phone call would most always spark some activity with Michael, which I found intriguing. Upon my arrival at the house for each visit the activity from the spirit would increase greatly.

During a recent conversation with Maxine, she told me that Michael had said to her that he was eight years old when he died. He also told her that he was born on August 8th, 1943. Once again, this caused me to believe even more that Michael was not a poltergeist, because of the many intelligent conversations between Maxine, Twyla, and Michael. In the renowned parapsychologists, Alan Gauld, and A.D. Cornell's book *Poltergeist*, Gauld says that "often times, many of the same phenomena exists in both cases of a poltergeist and a haunting, or spirit of the dead, and that we should not lump the two within the same category." Some of the phenomena includes, but is not limited to: conversations between the "Agent" and the spirit or poltergeist. While both spirits of the dead and poltergeists have much of the same common types of activity, they may not be the same entity.

In my opinion, there are only a handful of people in the world, who, with little or no effort, can attract spirits; Twyla is one of those people. Some spirits come and go however, there are those spirits who like Michael, will not leave. Most parapsychologists believe that PK or psycho kinesis, the ability to repress anger and hostility within the subconscious mind, may be the root of the manifestation within the "Agent." I do not believe that PK is prevalent in this particular case. Instead, I believe that Michael has found the family he has always wanted. Because Michael had died tragically at a young age, his spirit was not free to rest, but to roam the earth amongst the living. I truly think that when you have lived a full life, and then die, your work on earth has been completed and therefore free to be at peace. For Michael, he never had the chance to live his life and fulfill his dreams.

Based solely upon my experiences with the spirit Michael, and the testimony of the Mcwethy family and other witnesses to the haunting, I strongly believe that Michael's death was caused by his own father. I can only speculate as to how Michael died, but I believe he was drowned in a well, in Maxine's backyard. Once again, this is my opinion based upon the message that I received on my answering machine. I believe without any reservation that the message was intended for only me to hear. For some reason, Michael trusts me with the little bits of information that he gives me in one form, or another.

As for Leader, I could not find enough information to substantiate his presence in the house. If Leader is a violent spirit, maybe he was the spirit that ran Eric and I out of the house that night. It could be construed that Leader, the violent spirit, could be Michaels father and the two could be at war with each other in the house. Once again, these opinions are my own and may not be true; I can only rely on my own facts, and what I experienced in the house, to come to these conclusions. If Leader does in fact exist, and he is able to fully manifest himself, the Mcwethy family could be in serious danger. The night that Eric and I were run out of Maxine's house, I felt a different presence, unlike Michael's presence. I felt seriously threatened, and the activity more violent, than I had ever experienced. If we look at the whole picture, there maybe several spirits in the house.

While looking into the haunting at the Mcwethy home, I noticed several patterns developing when the strange events occurred: First, when Twyla was present at the house the activity was strongest. The activity would happen both, during the day, and night. However, there were many times when Twyla visited Maxine's house that there was little or no activity. I found that when Twyla was well rested and full of energy the strange activity was at its highest level, on the other hand, when she was tired and not feeling well, no activity from Michael occurred. This pattern led me to conclude that Michael must draw upon Twyla's energy in order to move objects around the house, or create other paranormal disturbances. The second pattern that I noticed when the strange activity started was that in most cases; only the male occupants of the house were attacked. Each time that I or another male in the house was talking to Twyla, the attacks on that particular male individual would sometimes become violent. When I use the term violent, I do no not use it in the text that the attacks are life threatening, but frequent, quick attacks involving little or no physical harm. An example of an attack would be: Suddenly being struck by an object such as a piece of silverware, a pot or pan, a rock or other similar items. I believe that Michael is jealous of any man who speaks to, or becomes close to Twyla. This part of my theory plays directly into the fact that Michael does not like males because it was a male, his father, who took his life at a young age.

Although this theory is just speculation only, it seems to make the most sense. I have had the opportunity to study the Mcwethy haunting for many years, which has allowed me to take an objective look at the spirit, Michael, from an occupant point of view. I was also able to study the activity from two thousand miles away because of the phone calls from Maxine, and messages that I had received from Michael. The bizarre events that have occurred, and continue to occur at Maxine's house, will I believe, last for many more years.

With this theory in mind, for me, there are only two questions that remain to be answered; why am I able to converse with the Spirit Michael? How large is my role in this particular case? I believe that my obsessive focus and interest in this case has made Michael curious as to what my intentions are. With that being said, I think Michael trusts my judgment, concerning my personal investigation into this case. That is why I think he gives me just enough information to keep me interested, and coming back to the house. In the beginning, when I first met the Mcwethy family, I was like anyone else who first visited the house; I was there to see a ghost! Now, seven years later, I finally realize how big my role has become.

Writing this book did not come without certain sacrifices, some of which, hit home emotionally. During my investigation of the Mcwethy home, and later, the writing of this book, a great deal of strain between my wife, and I, has surfaced. We have since separated because I have become consumed, and obsessed with this case. I have also become distant with relatives and friends. Their has been some good to this case as well; at forty-three years of age, I have finally found a life long interest in this type of work, and hope to investigate other cases in the future.

If you ever find yourself traveling down the dark lonesome stretch of highway 3W in Southeastern Oklahoma, you might want to pay a visit to 207 east First Street, in Centrahoma. Maxine will welcome you with a smile and hot cup of coffee, expect nothing to happen, but beware, be prepared for anything!

ABOUT THE AUTHOR

This being my first book, has taken my personal life to a different level. I had never been involved in a haunting or any paranormal activity before my encounter with the spirit "Michael." I had also been a hardened skeptic and steadfast non-believer when it came to the world of ghosts and spirits, but that all changed in November 1997. After spending more than seven years, investigating the haunting at the Mcwethy home and living in the house with the family during my investigation, I was compelled to write this book, during that time, my life had changed dramatically. I became so engrossed, and obsessed by the experience, that nothing else mattered. I continue to travel to different parts of the United States in search of more paranormal activity. I currently live in the state of Florida and continue to visit the Mcwethy home in southern Oklahoma, whenever possible.

www.ingramcontent.com/pod-product-compliance
Lightning Source LLC
Chambersburg PA
CBHW051420280526
45785CB00003B/1099